Chris Child's
Projects for Woodturners

Chris Child's
Projects for Woodturners

GUILD OF MASTER CRAFTSMAN PUBLICATIONS LTD

First published 2002 by
Guild of Master Craftsman Publications Ltd
166 High Street Lewes
East Sussex BN7 1XU

Reprinted 2003

Text and photographs © Chris Child 2002
(except author portrait by Tony Boase)
© in the work GMC Publications 2002
Drawings by Rob Wheele (pages 7, 13, 18, 38, 53, 71)
Kilnwood Graphics (pages 75, 78, 83, 86, 93, 96)
McBride Design (pages 99, 106, 108, 115)

ISBN 1 86108 269 X

A catalogue record for this book is available from the British Library.

Cover design by Ian Smith at GMC Publications design studio
Author portrait by Tony Boase; other photographs by Chris Child

Colour origination by Viscan Graphics (Singapore)
Printed and bound by Kyodo Printing (Singapore)

Contents

Warning

Although woodturning is safer than many other activities involving machinery, all machine work is inherently dangerous unless suitable precautions are taken.

Do not use timber which may come apart on the lathe – beware of faults such as dead knots, splits, shakes, loose bark, etc.

Avoid loose clothing or hair which may catch in machinery. Protect your eyes and lungs against dust and flying debris by wearing goggles, dust mask or respirator as necessary, but invest in an efficient dust extractor as well.

Pay attention to electrical safety; in particular, do not use wet sanding or other techniques involving water unless your lathe is designed so that water cannot come into contact with the electrics.

Keep tools sharp; blunt tools are dangerous because they require more pressure and may behave unpredictably.

Do not work when your concentration is impaired by drugs, alcohol or fatigue.

The safety advice in this book is intended for your guidance, but cannot cover every eventuality: the safe use of machinery and tools is the responsibility of the user. If you are unhappy with a particular technique or procedure, do not use it – there is always another way.

Measurements

Although care has been taken to ensure that the imperial measurements are true and accurate, they are only conversions from metric; they have been rounded up or down to the nearest ⅛in, or to the nearest convenient equivalent in cases where the metric measurements themselves are only approximate. When following the projects, use either the metric or the imperial measurements; do not mix units.

Introduction

Many people are shy of attempting to learn a hand skill from a book; it can be very difficult to grasp the necessary skills by simply seeing them described in writing. This is why, when I write about woodturning, I rely so much on clear pictures to get the message across, and why I go through the various procedures – such as the setting up of the workpiece, and the basic cutting techniques of the tools used – in such meticulous detail. But even with the best will in the world, I must admit that no book can substitute for the kind of knowledge gained from hands-on experience under the guidance of an experienced tutor.

This book contains a selection of popular woodturning projects that can be tackled on a basic lathe using standard tools and equipment, and is intended to help the kind of person who is attracted to woodturning but who may have had no previous experience of woodwork. It is meant to be taken into the workshop and placed at the back of the lathe, where it will lead you step by step through the various stages on the way to making a favourite woodturning project. With the book to accompany you, you will be helped through the difficulties that you encounter using the easiest and most effective methods that I know. The book explains what the likely problems will be, and suggests remedies to avoid them, and even ways to get you out of trouble when things do go wrong. With care and a methodical approach, by the time you have undertaken one or two of these projects you should be well on the way to mastering many of the skills and techniques of this fascinating craft.

Even if you have never handled a gouge before, you can embark straight away on one of the projects that takes your fancy, but if you are uneasy you might like to go through a simple exercise or two before you take the plunge. One that I start all my students on is that of securing a small round log firmly on the lathe and then, with a freshly sharpened gouge, reducing it to a pile of shavings on the floor.

Wood is a wonderful material to work with, and the woodturning lathe takes all the hard work out of cutting the material. It is a craft that is quick to give its rewards: most woodturning projects are completed in a day, and some can be realised from start to finish in an evening. It makes a relaxing and rewarding hobby after work. Many retired people take it up as a way to supplement their pension, and as a therapeutic work experience to keep a routine and structure their day – a bit of work on the lathe in the morning, and out to the craft shop or retailer to deliver their goods in the afternoon.

Chris Child
January 2002

Two-pounder

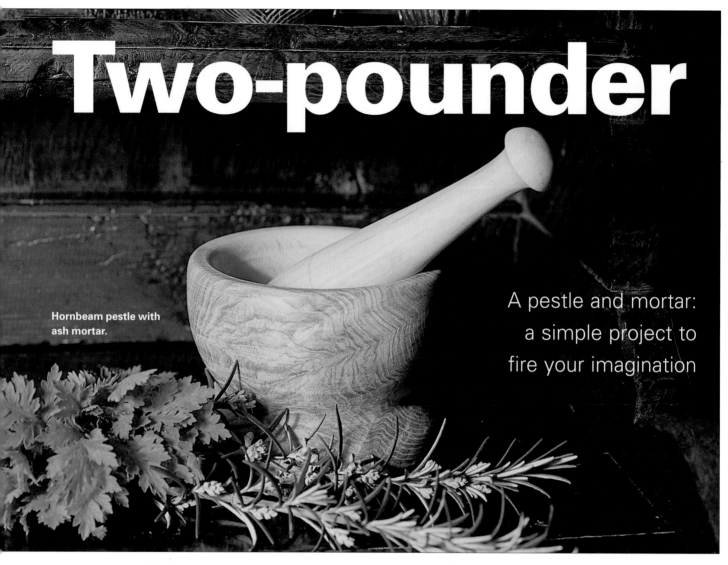

Hornbeam pestle with ash mortar.

A pestle and mortar: a simple project to fire your imagination

Some bits of kitchen equipment, like a pestle and mortar, are a joy to use, especially if you've made them yourself. The mortar bowl shown was made from 125mm (5in) square stock I'd been drying out slowly for three or four years.

Make sure the wood you use is equally well seasoned, to avoid the risk of the work splitting after completion, especially in centrally heated kitchens.

The mortar bowl design is different from the usual fruit or salad bowl, as its cavity is formed in the end-grain surface, whereas fruit and salad bowls are made from discs cut out of a board, and have the grain running sideways through their sections.

This gives the mortar a hard concave surface for the pestle to grind

against – but it makes hollowing the chamber more difficult.

To start, cut a 100mm (4in) long section of ash and mark the centres on the end-grain surfaces. Hammer a four-jaw drive centre into one end, using a copper-headed hammer to avoid damaging the drive centre's taper.

With a timber as hard as ash, the jaws of the centre will indent no more than 1mm (¾₄in) into the end grain. This supports and drives the work, while it is held in place by the revolving centre in the tailstock. I use a revolving tail centre for between-centre work, because it spins with the work and doesn't burn like the fixed or dead centres sometimes do.

Tighten the tailstock to hold the workpiece securely on the lathe. You can quickly test for tightness by

locking the headstock spindle and twisting the workpiece in your hand.

If the work turns round or becomes dislodged from its centres, it will need a few more turns of the tailstock hand wheel. Position the toolrest along the edge of the work so it is about 13mm (½in) below the centre of the workpiece.

Lathe speed

Run your lathe at a fast speed (e.g. 1200rpm) to turn off the corners of the 125mm (5in) square section. If you select a speed slower than 1000rpm, the gouge may move in and out of the work as it alternates from cutting away waste to open spaces, causing loss of control.

A lathe speed of 1360rpm worked well for me, but I wouldn't recommend you use anything faster.

Sharpening the roughing gouge.

Honing the roughing gouge flute with a slip stone.

Turn the block by hand to ensure the corners won't foul the toolrest when rotating. Check the toolrest levers and tailstock barrel locks are tight.

Stand clear before switching on the lathe, and do a brief test run. If there is too much vibration, you may need to reduce the speed a notch, but if all goes well you are ready to start turning. All you need is a sharp gouge.

Sharpening

I usually start with a 19mm (¾in) roughing gouge to cut off the corners and reduce the piece to a cylinder. It must be extra-sharp to produce a smooth, trouble-free cut. A blunt gouge will be hard work, and can hammer the workpiece and dislodge it from its centres. I use a bevel angle of

40°, but this is not critical. Many of the problems in woodturning are caused by badly ground and poorly sharpened tools. There are no short cuts.

Before sharpening your tools you need to get the grindstone into good cutting shape. Repeated use, especially with High-Speed-Steel tools, quickly clogs and dulls the edge of the wheel, so that instead of grinding, the stone simply rubs the edge of the tool, causing it to blue (burn).

I trim my wheel with a diamond-wheel dresser before every sharpening session to create a fresh cutting surface on the stone.

Sharpen the gouge by laying it flat on the dry grinder's tool support. Bring the bevel of the tool gently against the

grindwheel and rotate the tool so the whole edge is ground (photo 1).

A row of sparks will appear over the edge of the tool when it is getting sharp. At this stage examine the edge in a strong light for any signs of bluntness, such as a surface shine on the extreme tip, or marks from previous use still on the bevel.

When satisfied you have produced a fresh edge, finish by running a slip-stone along the inside of the flute (photo 2). This improves the edge by pushing the tiny serrations or burr caused by the grinding, outwards.

Another method of testing the sharpness of a ground tool is to run your finger carefully over the edge. It should feel slightly serrated like the teeth of a minute saw.

Tools and timbers

9.5mm (⅜in) beading and parting tool.

19mm (¾in) roughing gouge.

6mm (¼in) bowl gouge.

13mm (½in) round scraper.

1.5mm (⅛6in) parting tool.

Vernier callipers.

Ash, 125 x 125 x 150mm
    (5 x 5 x 6in).

Hornbeam, 45 x 45 x 180mm
    (1¾ x 1¾ x 7in).

Chuck, with 75mm (3in) jaws.

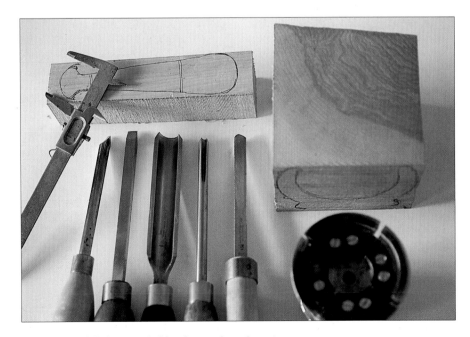

The tools and timber needed for the pestle and mortar.

Cutting with the parting tool at a 45° angle.

Slice-cutting with the bowl gouge.

Wear eye and face shields when turning down square-section stock to a cylinder, as it's quite likely to splinter. Also, when turning between centres you are much more vulnerable to particles flying in your direction, due to your working position.

Also protect your lungs from wood dust with a suitable face mask, extraction system or respirator.

Stand facing the lathe so you can move freely from side to side, while anchoring the gouge handle to your body. Rest the blade of the tool on the toolrest and slowly bring the edge into the path of the corners of the work as it revolves.

Shallow cuts

Hold the tool down firmly onto the toolrest, but don't grip it too tight or push it into the work. Any pressure exerted should be directed downwards, onto the toolrest. Use shallow cuts and gradually reduce the diameter.

Avoid taking deep cuts, as they will cause the tool to snatch out of control and skid along the toolrest. From time to time, look at the top edge of the work to check your progress.

As you work, a space will open up between the toolrest and the work surface, which you will need to close now and then by moving the toolrest in. The closer the toolrest to the work surface, the more leverage you can exert and the more control you will have over the tool.

Prepare the work so it can be held at one end in a chuck. I use the Master-chuck with 75mm (3in) accessory jaws, which need a dovetail spigot on

the end of the work. Use a pair of vernier callipers to measure the inside diameter of the jaws, and cut the spigot to size using a 10mm (⅜in) beading and parting tool. This is just a strong square-sectioned chisel ground on both sides to form a diamond point.

For this tool to perform properly it needs a better class of edge than is normally needed by the gouge. Regular honing on the oilstone will enable it to cut cleanly and accurately.

To form a spigot 6mm (¼in) long on the end of the workpiece, present the beading and parting tool at a 45° cutting angle and feed it slowly into the work so it removes the waste in a fine shaving (photo 3).

The dovetail is made by turning the tool on its side and using the diamond shape of the tool to scrape a small V-cut in the shoulder of the spigot.

Lower the toolrest and hold the beading tool with the tip pointing to the work in a slightly downward, scraping angle.

Facing off

With the workpiece held in the chuck, you no longer need the support of the tailstock, and can work freely on the end surface of the work. Before hollowing the bowl it's a good idea to square the end to form a smooth, even surface to work on.

I use a small 6mm (¼in) bowl gouge to face off the end, as it puts less pressure on the work and produces a cleaner finish than a parting cut. Sharpen this deep-fluted gouge in the same way as the roughing gouge.

Use a slicing or shearing cut, which

means starting the cut at the corner of the work, with the bevel of the gouge lined up with the direction of the cut. The toolrest is positioned at 45° to the work.

The gouge travels across the work-face, removing a small section of about 1mm (³⁄₆₄in) at a time. The bevel glides on the freshly cut surface like the sole of a plane, with the edge at the base of the gouge's flute creating the slicing action (photo 4).

Critical part

The critical part of the operation is when the bevel of the gouge is unsupported at the start of the cut. Take special care at this point, and use a very slow feeding action while holding it firmly down against the toolrest. Once you are past this difficult point, you can relax and let the gouge take over and guide itself across.

The simplest way to hollow end grain is with a scraper. I put an extra-long 760mm (30in) handle on my 13mm (½in) round-nosed scraper, designed for tackling deep hollows like the one in this mortar.

I grind the bevel to an angle of about 60°, and have also formed a smaller 10mm (⅜in) radius on my 13mm (½in) scraper.

This reduces the surface area of the cut, which might otherwise lead to an overloading of the tool and result in the work coming off the chuck.

Adjust the toolrest so the scraper, when pointed slightly downwards at a scraping angle, cuts the centre point of the workface. Start cutting at the

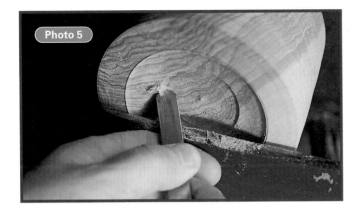

Cutting outwards from the centre with the scraper.

Keeping the bevel in line with the curve.

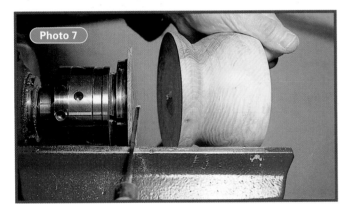

Parting off the mortar.

Turning down the corners with the roughing gouge.

centre and work backwards towards the outer edge of the bowl.

Push the nose of the tool into the work and try to cut through the fibres at the base of their support with a sideways hooking or scooping action. Don't forget to keep the scraper flat on the rest, using it as the fulcrum of the arch (photo 5).

Slide the headstock along the bed-bars to the end of the lathe bed, so you can hold the tool handle close to your body. You have much more control over the work this way, rather than having to hold it out at arms' stretch.

Simple depth gauge

Use a simple depth gauge to test the depth of the cavity. Make the gauge from a piece of dowel pushed through a hole in a cross stretcher.

Stop the lathe from time to time to close the gap over the toolrest, keeping the gap down to 13mm (½in) if possible. I changed to a shorter rest, angled along the wall of the bowl.

I did all the hollowing out with one

tool, to a depth of about 55mm (2¼in). The distance across the top of the opening was about 95mm (3¾in).

The sides were 13mm (½in) thick and the sweep of the inside curve of the bowl continuous, all the way from the floor to the top edge of the bowl, where the lip was later rounded.

The outside shape

I formed the outer shape of the bowl with a 6mm (¼in) bowl gouge. The ash grain was particularly twisty and needed the same slice-cutting technique as when facing off. Notice how fine my cut is on the side of the bowl, with the bevel kept in line with the curve (photo 6).

The finish needs very little sanding, because the wood fibres have not been cut at right angles, but sliced through at an angle, causing minimum disturbance.

Use a heavier cut on the base area of the bowl, in the opposite direction to the previous cut. To form the base of the hollow in the side of the mortar,

twist the tool to bring the bottom of its flute into play. Due to the inevitable gap over the toolrest, use the finest of cuts to trim away the last untidy traces of where the two curves meet.

Sand the work by going through the different grades of abrasive cloth. I started with a coarse 80-grit aluminium oxide which removed tool marks, followed by 150-grit which removed the marks of the previous abrasive, and ended with 400-grit.

Parting off

Finally, part off with a freshly sharpened parting tool. I use a 1.5mm (¹⁄₁₆in) parting tool, ground and honed square across at the end. Cut the groove extra wide when you part off, so the tool doesn't get restricted and overheated as it would in a single-width cut.

Make sure you undercut the work so the mortar sits squarely on its outer rim. You can part all the way through if you are feeling very brave (photo 7), or take the easier and safer option of

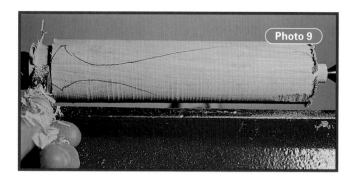

Reducing the diameter with the parting tool.

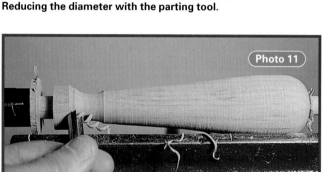

Cutting off the corner of the workpiece.

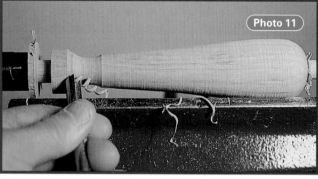

Creating the small radius in the base of the handle.

Rounding off.

stopping the lathe and hand-sawing the last 13mm (½in) or so.

Even if it is a little extra work to trim the base with a chisel, it's probably a sounder method in the long run.

The pestle

The pestle is made from a block of seasoned hornbeam, 180 x 45 x 45mm (7 x 1¾ x 1¾in) square. This is a very hard, dense-grained wood, which turns beautifully and is quite odourless, making it ideal for food utensils.

Mount the block between centres and turn the corners down with the roughing gouge. Hold the tool in to the body, with the same angle of approach as in photo 8.

Mark out the top and bottom of the pestle, leaving 13mm (½in) or so at either end as waste. With the beading and parting tool, cut down on the outside of the lines and reduce the diameter of the waste to about 13mm (½in) (photo 9).

This gives you a space to work into when you round off the top and bottom of the pestle. It also helps support the work while the middle

section is being shaped. Give the beading and parting tool an extra hone on the oilstone to get the edge back to 100% sharpness, and begin rounding the top of the pestle.

Position the tool so the blade is resting flat against the top surface of the cylinder, at the end of the workpiece, about 6mm (¼in) from the edge.

Twist the tool so the corner of the blade engages with the work, lifting the fibres slightly. Continue rolling the tool over, so the corner of the workpiece is cut off (photo 10).

Replace the tool a little way to the left of the previous cut and repeat the operation until a full half-round has been formed.

Use the same operation to form the butt of the pestle's handle.

The secret of forming a round shape with the beading and parting tool is to use only the tip of the corner of the tool's edge to do the cutting, to take very fine cuts, and have lots and lots of practice.

This is one of the most difficult turning tasks to master, and you won't be the first person to reduce your work

to a series of spiral gashes if your attempts go astray.

However, when you get the hang of it, you will be able to achieve, quickly and efficiently, the kind of professional finish that is the stamp of the fully skilled woodturner.

With the small 6mm (¼in) bowl gouge, create the small radius in the base of the handle (photo 11), and use the roughing gouge, with its broader flute, to shape the gentle curve of the middle section of the pestle.

Parting cuts

Part off the work with the beading and parting tool, using a combination of parting cuts to reduce the thickness of the waste section, followed by a series of slicing cuts with the corner of the tool, following the same principles as above, for rounding off (photo 12).

Decorate as you wish, before sanding, while there is still enough waste material to support the work. Then slice off the work, holding the beading tool in one hand and cradling the wood in the other.

A touch of hand sanding is all that remains to finish off. ■

Basic box

Box making was a favourite project of the 'gentleman woodturner' in the 19th century. He would have spent hours at his ornamental treadle lathe, making an assortment of intricate snuff and pill boxes out of precious woods such as tulipwood, rosewood and lignum vitae.

It is still enjoyed today, probably because boxes are usually one-offs which can be made in almost any shape and size. There is lots of scope for creativity and improvising with the design.

Suitable timbers to start box making are sycamore, yew, English maple and cherry – but you can use practically any wood. My example is

This simple lidded box is an ideal project for beginners

made from very dark brown oak, coloured by a common fungus. It was made from seasoned wood, so there was no need to take measures to prevent splitting, as is often the case with semi-seasoned wood.

Chucking and mounting

To make a box, you need to find a way of securing your wood to the lathe at one end, so you can work at the other end, free from obstructions. You can achieve this without a chuck, by doing some preparation work the night before. Glue your block of wood to a disc of scrap plywood, and when the glue has set, you can use your faceplate, screwed to the back of the waste plywood disc, to mount the work onto the lathe.

Using the chuck method, you will need to turn your block of wood down to a cylinder between centres first. Take your block, mark out the centres at each end, drive a two- or four-pronged centre into one end by

Fig. 1

30mm (1⅛in)

4mm (⁵⁄₃₂in)

4mm (⁵⁄₃₂in)

8mm (⁵⁄₁₆in)

7mm (⁹⁄₃₂in)

130mm (5⅛in)

90mm (3½in)

10mm (⅜in)

7mm (⁹⁄₃₂in)

7mm (⁹⁄₃₂in)

12mm (½in)

15mm (⁹⁄₁₆in)

110mm (4⅜in)

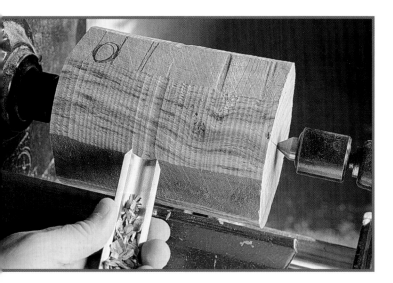

Turn the block to a cylinder with a sharp roughing gouge.

Use the beading and parting tool on its side like a scraper, to form the dovetail.

tapping it with a soft-headed hammer, and mount the work on the lathe between centres.

Set the toolrest 19mm (¾in) below centre, and as close as you can without it interfering with the rotation of the work. The lathe must be set at a fairly fast speed of about 1000rpm – don't forget to wear your face mask.

Turn the block to a cylinder with a sharp roughing gouge. Form a dovetail at one end, so it can be gripped in a Masterchuck by first cutting a 6mm (¼in) long spigot at one end of the cylinder with a beading and parting tool.

Then, with the tool on its side, use it like a scraper and form the dovetail with the diamond tip. To do this you must lower the toolrest and hold the beading tool with the tip slanting slightly downward – a scraping angle – to the work.

Fit the work securely in the chuck and clean off the face of the cylinder with a small ¼in (6mm) bowl gouge, used with the bevel floating parallel with the direction of cut so that the cutting edge slices cleanly through the end fibres. This tool, by taking off fine shavings, will produce a silky-smooth finish and exerts the least leverage on the workpiece.

Making the lid

The inside of the lid is formed first. Use a small 13mm (½in) round-nosed scraper to hollow. Holding it horizontally, start cutting in the centre of the workface and work towards the edge by slowly gyrating the tool, using a fixed point on the toolrest as the axis point. In this way the edge of the tool cuts from behind the fibres of the wood, removing them by the roots.

In the lid's edge, cut a square 6mm (¼in) rebate with the beading and parting tool. This should be perfectly straight and parallel. It will be needed to locate the lid on the box's body.

Make sure that your parting tool is perfectly square with very sharp corners, and cut your rebate in a series of small cuts to avoid vibration, as this will result in the lid fitting off-centre.

Measure the depth of the hollow in the lid and mark it on the side of the work. Add about 6mm (¼in) for the thickness of the lid and more for any knob or finial you want to include.

Clean the face of the cylinder with a ¼in (6mm) bowl gouge.

Use a fixed point on the toolrest as the point of axis, so the tool cuts from behind the fibres, removing them by the roots.

Part off the lid section here, using a freshly sharpened parting tool. I use a 1.5mm (¹⁄₁₆in) parting tool, ground and then honed square across the end.

Cut the groove extra wide when you part off, so that the tool doesn't get restricted and overheated, as it would do in a single-width cut. Part down until it can be broken off when the lathe is stopped, or safely sawn through if you prefer.

Drill a hole in the body of the box with a 25mm (1in) saw-tooth bit to provide a starting place for hollowing, and also to fix the depth of the box. Allow about 25mm (1in) of thickness to accommodate the floor, the width

Cut a square ¼in (6mm) rebate in the edge of the lid, using the beading and parting tool.

Part off the lid with a ¹⁄₁₆in (1.5mm) parting tool, ground and then honed square across the end.

Drill a hole in the body with a 25mm (1in) saw-tooth bit to provide a starting place for hollowing.

Scrape a recess into the face of the body with a square-ended scraper.

of the parting cut and the 6mm (¼in) waste section needed to hold the work in the chuck when it is finally parted off.

The knob and the outside shape of the lid are turned with the lid jammed onto the body of the box. To do this, carefully scrape a recess into the face of the body with a square-end scraper, for the lid to jam onto.

I use a square scraper for this, which has had its side edge ground back on a wet stone, and then honed till the edge is chisel-sharp. This is so that it does not bind against the concave surface that it is working against.

The precise sizing of the recess of the body to the rebate on the lid is crucial to the latter's successful completion. If you cut a little too much off the body, the lid can pop out

when you try to turn it; but cut not enough and you risk splitting the sides of the box when you try to jam in the lid.

Knob or finial

With the lid secured, you can finish turning the parts that had been inaccessible before. I shape the lid's dome by taking fine slicing cuts with the ¼-inch (6mm) bowl gouge. These are repeated until the waste area from the top sides of the lid has been removed and a spigot left to form the knob.

As your cuts come close to the small waist of the knob, change over and take even finer cuts with the 10mm (⅜in) spindle gouge. The small spindle gouge with its long side edges can slice through end-grain fibres and produce

To make the dome of the lid, take fine slicing cuts with the ¼in (6mm) bowl gouge.

As your cuts come close to the small waist of the knob, change over and take even finer cuts with the 10mm (⅜in) spindle gouge.

Use the bowl gouge as you did when forming the top of the lid, to flatten the crown on the knob.

a very clean finish. It's the only tool with a small enough point to form the small, deep hollow of the knob's waist.

Place the toolrest as close as possible to the work for these very delicate cuts to the lid and knob, because you will need all the control you can get. A split-second lack of concentration and the tool can slip laterally and damage be done. This lateral slipping of the tool can be avoided through a combination of applying firm pressure on the tool to anchor it onto the toolrest and taking

only the finest of cuts, especially when cutting with the tool on its side. Use the bowl gouge in the same way as you did when forming the top of the lid, to flatten the crown of the knob.

The box's body

When you make the body of the box, leave the lid fitted, as this enables you to see the box's form and proportions as a whole. I usually leave the body design fairly plain, especially if the lid is very ornate.

The sides are smoothed with the roughing gouge, which will produce an adequate finish on side grain, so long as it's sharp and a fine cut is taken. If a few ripples remain, they are easily removed with the first touch of abrasive.

I have put a small bead at the top of the side of the box and one near the base of the box. These were done by first making a pair of shallow V-cuts with the point of a 13mm (½in) skew chisel on each side of where the bead is to be made.

Hold the tool on its side with the longer side down, position the point at the angle you want the chamfer of the V-cut to be, and start slicing.

Cut a thin slice off one side, repeat the same action on the other side, and slowly form a V-cut to the size you want. I formed the round convex curve of the bead by nibbling the corners off with the side of the tool.

The final rounding off of the bead is left to the sanding stage. I know this is

not the accepted way to create a bead, but so long as the tool is sharp it's an effective method.

Sand the outside of the box smooth using some fresh abrasive, taking care not to lose any precious detail. Start with a fairly coarse 100-grit J-Flex aluminium-oxide abrasive, which should remove all the tool marks.

Do the final shaping stage of the beads by sanding off the little facets left by the skew chisel. Follow this with 240 grit and finish off with 400 grit.

At each sanding stage, carefully remove the sanding marks of the previous abrasive before going on to the next stage.

Add polish

When you are satisfied that there are no marks on the box other than the natural figure of the grain, you can add your polish. If you've correctly done the previous stages, almost any coat of oil, varnish, sealer or shellac will produce a beautiful finish.

But if there are still scuff marks on the work from a tool snatch, or bruises where the end grain has been disturbed, even scratches left from the coarse abrasive that have not been cleaned up, no amount of polishing will remedy these faults. It can be a cruel shock to find such marks on your work when you are so close to completion, but it's often only when the polish has been applied that these faults appear. When this happens to me, I use up my old worn-out abrasives to remove the polish, before going through the sanding stages again.

One of the simplest finishes to apply is soft wax. A wide selection is now available, some using fast-drying solvents ideal for turned work.

The lathe's rotation enables the surface to be quickly burnished, and any surplus wax rubs off onto the polishing cloth.

The finer and closer-grained woods like boxwood, rosewood, and many of the common fruitwoods, respond well to the harder carnauba-wax finishes, while coarser-grained woods such as elm, oak and some open-grained mahogany substitutes are better left matt or given a soft sheen.

I know many woodturners don't consider a box to be properly finished until every surface is smooth and flawless, but I prefer to leave the inside free from polish, and sometimes not even sanded.

This is not just because it's nearly impossible to create a satisfactory finish on the inside floor of a box, but because it creates a nice contrast to see what the wood looks like in its natural state, in contrast to the polished surface of the outside. There may also be hygienic reasons for keeping the inside of the box unpolished if food products are to be stored inside.

Hollowing the box

A scraper is often the most effective method of hollowing boxes and other hollow vessels, where it's impossible to use other standard cutting tools.

Remove most of the waste using the scraper in a forward motion, sliding it down the side of the pre-drilled hole like a reamer. By feeding the scraper along the side of the hole made by the drill and only removing a small amount of wood at a time, slowly open the hole to the required width.

The full width of the scraper's cutting edge must be prevented from biting into the floor of the box at all costs, as this will cause a tremendous snatch and may dislodge the workpiece.

To make beads at the top and bottom of the box, first make a pair of shallow V-cuts with the point of a 13mm (½in) skew chisel.

Remove most of the waste by using the scraper in a forward motion, sliding it down the side of the pre-drilled hole like a reamer.

Parting off the body of the box.

To cut the floor of the box, move the side of the scraper laterally across the floor, cutting away less than a millimetre at a time, with the sharpened outer side of the tool. Only the extreme corner of the scraper's edge is used. This will need repeated sharpening to keep it working efficiently.

To perform the same operation on the floor, it's essential to have a long handle on your tool, to exert the leverage needed when cutting deep inside the container. Make sure the lid's tight fit is eased a bit before finally parting off the box. Use the standard parting-tool technique and remember to dish the cut into the base of the work so that the finished box will sit fair and square on its outer rim. The base can be finished by hand or covered with a piece of baize. ■

Perfectly simple

How to make a simple but beautiful fruit bowl from a piece of English cherry

Cherry bowl.

I made this fruit bowl from a perfect piece of English cherry. It had been air-dried for three or four years so that it wouldn't split or warp in the dry environment of the home.

To help me find the centre of the bowl blank, I made a simple device from Perspex, scoring a series of radiating circles with dividers.

With this useful tool, the centre of even the most irregular bowl blank can be quickly found by sighting the circle closest to the circumference of the blank.

I then fixed a faceplate to the blank using four size 10 screws, which penetrated about 13mm (½in) into the surface – far enough on sound wood. If the screws spin round at the end of their travel, use longer ones.

When you've fitted the bowl to the lathe, check that it's secure by slapping the back of the blank with the palm of the hand. If it stays solid, with no detectable gap between faceplate and bowl, it's safe to go on.

Now select a suitable lathe speed. If you are not used to turning large diameters on your lathe, try the slowest speed first and then, if this seems a little slow, raise the speed a notch. I found 625rpm worked well for everything – turning, sanding and polishing.

When turning bowls or other hollow vessels, it helps to have a lathe with a swivelling headstock, so the work can be rotated at 90° to the lathe bed, allowing easier access to the work. I used an alternative arrangement, positioning the headstock nearly at the end of the lathe's bed bars, leaving just enough space for the toolrest support.

It means I can stand in a safe, comfortable, well-balanced position to the workpiece, without having to stretch awkwardly across the lathe bed or having to compromise with the cutting angle of the tools.

Before starting the lathe, check that the blank misses obstructions such as the toolrest. Stand well clear of the line of rotation and give the bowl a quick test-run, keeping your finger on the switch in case a problem occurs.

Your lathe will probably wobble or vibrate at first because the blank is not fully concentric. Listen for tell-tale rattling sounds that indicate a lever is loose. Wear a face shield, as the speed generated at the rim of the disc is

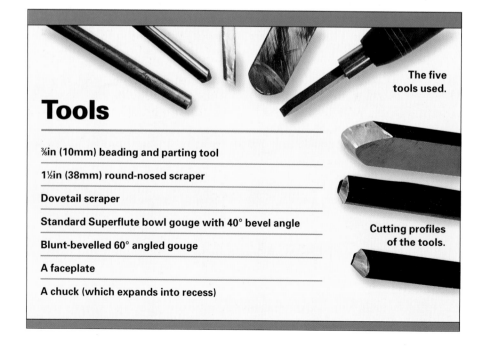

The five tools used.

Cutting profiles of the tools.

Tools

⅜in (10mm) beading and parting tool

1½in (38mm) round-nosed scraper

Dovetail scraper

Standard Superflute bowl gouge with 40° bevel angle

Blunt-bevelled 60° angled gouge

A faceplate

A chuck (which expands into recess)

Using a Perspex centre finder.

The headstock is positioned nearly at the end of the lathe's bed bars.

much faster than on spindle work.

I used the two-stage method to turn this bowl. It involves shaping the bottom of the bowl first, then reversing it and hollowing out the cavity with it held in a chuck.

The main advantage is that when turning the sides, the cut goes with the grain, leaving the fibres unruffled and smooth.

When it's turned in one stage, the turner has to cut the sides in the opposite direction, going against the grain. This results in the fibres being bent back on themselves, causing a rough finish.

The two-stage method calls for the addition of a beading and parting tool and a specially ground scraper for forming the dovetail recess for the chuck jaws to grip into.

I also use another bowl gouge, ground with a 60° bevel, as an alternative to the big round-nosed scraper, which is usually used for cleaning the floor of the bowl.

Preparing the gouge

A ½in (13mm) bowl gouge is an ideal tool for this project. I ground the bevel with a 40° angle, efficient both for removing waste and producing a superb finish. The bevel must be kept flat and free from secondary facets, as it performs like the sole of a plane, gliding on the surface of the work, while the cutting edge cuts a pre-determined section of waste away.

I've made a wooden platform for my wet grinder which, used with a stepped-wedge jig to find the same angle of the tool each time, enables me to instantly find the correct angle for sharpening each tool.

After grinding on the wet stone, hone the inside flute with a slipstone.

Turning left-handed

Although I'm right-handed, I hold the gouge left-handed to cut the bowl's base and side. This enables me to look down the back of the tool and judge the angle of the bevel in relation to the work surface.

I can also see the precise point at which the tool's cutting edge contacts the work. Because the left hand anchors the tool handle against the body and right hand is positioned between the back of the tool and the work, most of the pressure on the tool is exerted downwards onto the toolrest. This helps avoid the tendency to press the bevel too strongly against the work, causing uneven cutting and leading to a ripple, or wave, effect on the work's surface.

I use the stronger overhand grip when turning troublesome grain or at the start of a job. But once I'm confident of the terrain, I hold the tool underhand with my fingers. This allows a smoother movement of the tool.

More importantly, I can control the depth and feed of cut much more easily, as I can see the end of the tool. With the overhand grip the shavings are often trapped at the back of the hand, hiding the cutting point.

Turning the sides

The best way to shape the base is to cut away the corner first, forming a simple facet which can later be rounded to form the curved sides of the bowl. Hold the gouge firmly against the toolrest, slightly on its side, with the bevel in line with the face of the work surface.

Start by re-angling the gouge so the cutting edge touches the work at the base of the flute. The tool must be held rock solid in the path of the wood and not be influenced by the uneven surface.

After each pass of the disc, start a

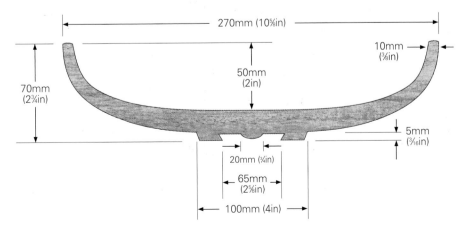

270mm (10⅝in)

70mm (2¾in)

50mm (2in)

10mm (⅜in)

5mm (³⁄₁₆in)

20mm (¾in)

65mm (2⅝in)

100mm (4in)

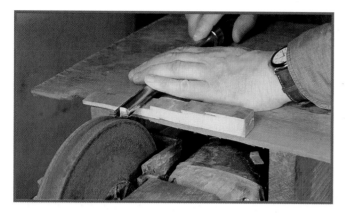

The wooden platform for the wet grinder, used with a step-wedge jig for angle finding.

Hold the gouge firmly against the toolrest, slightly on its side with the bevel in line with the work face.

fresh cut slightly behind the start of the previous one. The gouge slices through the wood fibres at their base and breaks them away at the side in one continuous action, while the bevel glides over the smooth new surface. As you proceed, remember to move the toolrest nearer the work to keep control of the cut.

To form the bowl's curved sides with one continuous cut, slowly swing the gouge in an arc, keeping the bevel parallel with the curve.

To do this while still supporting the tool handle against your body, stand in the position where you expect to end your cut, lean back to start the cut slightly stretched and off-balance, and slowly move back into a balanced position as you finish the cut. (This, I'm told, is the method golfers use to

maintain balance during their swing.)

Subsequent cuts to improve and modify the shape can be made by slicing off fine fillets. Start with the bevel flat on the surface and feather the edge of the gouge into the surface so no entry or exit sign is visible at the start or end of the cut. A scraper can be used to shape the outside of the bowl, but this tool will usually undo the clean finish produced by previous slicing work with the gouge, causing two broken or roughed-up areas where the surface has been scraped in the wrong direction.

The best finish is achieved with a freshly sharpened gouge, used as for the continuous shaping cut, but cut much more finely with a slower rate of feed.

Once you've shaped the sides, work on the base. I've formed a foot or plinth on my bowl by taking the sides a few cuts deeper and forming a shallow shoulder.

The sides of the foot are formed with the bowl gouge, and a beading and parting tool is used to clean out the corner.

To clean and flatten the base, drag the gouge against the side of the parallel toolrest, using a simple cutting angle like that used when roughing down a spindle.

Ensure there is at least a 19mm (¾in) border around the dovetail recess to hold the chuck's expansion jaws safely.

Dovetail recess

I used the Masterchuck to hold my bowl, but whatever make you use you will need to measure the outside diameter of the jaws with callipers, with the chuck in the closed position.

Cut the recess in the bowls's base with a ⅜in (10mm) beading and parting tool. Place the tool at a cutting angle of 45° to the work surface and hold it firmly down on the toolrest, to

As you proceed, move the toolrest nearer the work to keep control of the cut.

Clean and flatten the base.

Improve the shape by slicing off fine fillets.

Cut a recess in the base with a ⅜in (10mm) parting tool, held at a 45° angle to the work surface.

Use a specially ground scraper to cut the dovetail

keep it rigid during cutting. Any vibration will affect the centring of the bowl when it comes to be fitted onto the chuck.

The dovetail is cut with a specially ground scraper which forms the same profile cut as the chuck jaws. As with the beading and parting tool, it's essential to keep it absolutely rigid while it shapes the dovetail.

Apply decoration of your choice to disguise the utilitarian appearance of the dovetail recess at this stage, so long as it doesn't alter the effectiveness of the grip. Test that the chuck fits properly by hand-tightening it into the recess. Rotate the lathe to make sure it is centring correctly.

Sanding

Wear an effective dust mask when sanding. Indeed you should really wear one for the whole bowl-making process. I sand most of my turnings with J-flex aluminum-oxide cloth abrasive, as it's long-lasting and flexible enough for both outside and the more difficult curves inside.

I begin with 100 grit and work through to 240, ending with 400 grit. Use each grade to remove the scratch marks of the previous one.

Aim not just to smooth the surface, but also to remove tool marks. They usually only become visible when you are using the finer grades of abrasive. You may have to go over your work again with the coarse grit to remove a stubborn blemish too deep to be

removed with the fine or medium grit.

Don't use blunt abrasive, as this will often cause the fine end-grain cracking which can spoil an otherwise perfect piece. Change your abrasive often, to avoid burnishing the work, which should have a light, chalky look when finished.

Hollowing the bowl

Fit the chuck to the lathe first, and then the bowl to the chuck. Ensure the bowl is tight and well bedded, centrally on the chuck.

Before hollowing your bowl, flatten the face with the freshly sharpened bowl gouge in the way you flattened the base. The bowl is now at its most vulnerable, and can easily be dislodged from the chuck by a heavy cut or loss of tool control. Take very light cuts and keep a keen edge on your gouge, remembering that you are cutting an uneven surface which may well be ingrained with dust and abrasive grit.

Hollowing stages

Hollow the bowl in three stages. First cut the full depth of the hollow, leaving a floor thickness of about 19mm (¾in). To create an entry cut, position the gouge on its side with the bevel at a 45° lateral angle to the work surface.

Hold the tool at a 45° vertical cutting angle and adjust the height of the toolrest so the cutting edge, slightly to one side of the base of the flute, contacts the centre of the bowl

Fit the chuck to the lathe first, and then the bowl to the chuck. Make sure it's tight.

Create a conical cavity.

A vertical toolpost, made from a masonry nail placed in a hole in the toolrest, helps when cutting the edge of the bowl.

Test the thickness of the sides with your fingers after each cut.

Use a scraper to smoothly curve the lower section of the sides and inside floor area.

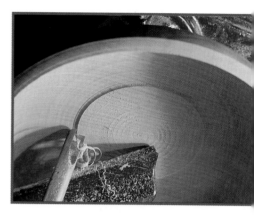

The 60° bevelled gouge can slide across the bowl's floor on its bevel and cut the wood fibres more clearly than the scraper.

face. Make the cut and then repeat it one step back. Keep cutting in this way, feeding the gouge into the centre of the bowl each time. This produces a conical cavity which you can test for depth with a simple depth gauge.

Stage two is to define the thickness of the lip of the bowl. Carry on taking 45° hollowing cuts until you have moved from the centre of the bowl and have the desired rim thickness.

I used a vertical toolpost, made from a masonry nail placed in a hole in the toolrest, to cut the edge of the bowl.

All that remains is to smoothly shape the bowl's inside. Concentrate on the rim first, and place a vertical toolpost in position to help you form a crisp, clean edge to the rim. This vertical post could be in the form of a piece of waste wood G-cramped to the rest, or the masonry nail mentioned earlier.

The toolpost gives rigid support at the back of the gouge, allowing it to be fed into the rim of the bowl at a 90° lateral angle without slipping and spoiling the crispness of the edge.

Arc the gouge in a lateral plane while feeding the edge forward and form the sides of the bowl, testing the thickness between your fingers after each cut.

The area where the curve of the sides meets the floor of the bowl needs particular care. It's more easily achieved using the ½in (13mm) round-nosed scraper with a 60° bevel. By holding a freshly ground

scraper horizontal and flat on the toolrest you can scrape the lower section of the sides and inside floor area so they form a smooth, continuous curve.

Another method of forming the bowl's inside curve, and one that produces a superior finish, is to use the standard 40° bowl gouge.

When the sides of the bowl obstruct the gouge's angle of approach, continue cutting the line of the curve using a gouge with a 60° bevel angle. This tool, because of its steeper bevel angle, can slide across the floor of the bowl on its bevel and cut the wood fibres more cleanly than the scraper, without making broken areas of end grain.

When sanding, fold the abrasive into a smaller pad than you used on the outside of the bowl; then it can be brought up to the corners of the rim without rounding them off. Otherwise, follow the same procedure as before.

Polishing

When the surface is perfectly smooth and free from any marks other than the grain, seal it with polish.

For a wood as beautiful as cherry, only the best finish will do.

I use traditional French polish, wiped on with the lathe stationary, using a piece of clean, cotton, flannelette shirt. I apply a coat or two and leave it to dry for 10 minutes before rubbing a soft, fast-drying Briwax, or its equivalent, over the bowl. Burnish to a soft, even shine.

This finish is not resistant to water or heat like most modern plastic finishes, but with further waxing it will mature and improve with age, becoming translucent and taking on a patina just like a piece of antique furniture. ■

For a wood as beautiful as cherry, only the best finish will do.

Make a mug tree

Test your spindle-turning skills with this three-legged mug tree

You can buy mug trees in the shops, but few of them compare with what can be made with a little ingenuity and basic spindle-turning skills, in your own workshop.

Space out the positions of the mug supports by suspending a standard-size mug by its handle, and marking out the positions on the side of a suitable piece of wood. Then, roughly sketch your design for the centre column of the mug tree on the sides of the block.

Be adventurous

I tend to use traditional designs, but you can be as adventurous as you like. My mug tree consists of a series of three pear shapes, separated by hollows called scotias and small square bands called fillets. The finial at the top of the column, which serves as a carrying handle, is in the form of a flattened ball or bun, above a scotia and fillet. At the very top of the

With the tripod mug tree, even wet surfaces in the kitchen are no problem.

finial, above the bun, is a small ogee-shaped cap.

The centre column is supported on tripod legs, which give stability and prevent the mug tree body from contacting wet or damp kitchen surfaces. Nine mug branches are fitted in sets of three, at a slight upward angle to the column.

I cut the deep-moulded shapes on the mug-tree's column with a 6mm (¼in) bowl gouge and 10mm (⅜in) beading and parting tool. A roughing gouge

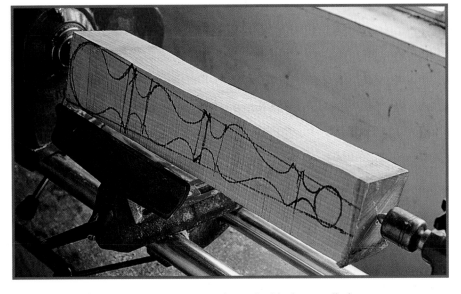

Fit your block of wood between centres and turn the block to a cylinder.

Tools

6mm (¼in) HSS bowl gouge

10mm(⅜in) beading and parting tool
10mm (⅜in) spindle gouge
(ground to lady's-fingernail shape)

was used to remove the bulk of the waste and make some of the broader curves.

A 6mm (¼in) bowl gouge is my favourite tool for slicing across end grain areas and forming deep, curved shapes. I sharpen it with a single, 40° bevel and grind the sides of the gouge back slightly to form a short, round nose. After grinding on the wet or dry stone, I hone the edge on a slipstone held flat against the inside of the flute. The gouge's fairly small, but deep, flute has little effect on the overall strength and rigidity of the tool, and the cut it makes is small enough to be controlled, even when stretching beyond the direct support of the toolrest.

You might be forgiven for thinking all 6mm (¼in) HSS bowl gouges are the same, but there is a surprising variety of different flute shapes, made for different purposes.

The 10mm (⅜in) beading and parting tool must be ground with matching long bevels, so that it looks like a well-sharpened pencil. The cutting edge has to be ground square across with pristine corners, after which it should be honed on the oilstone until razor-sharp.

Centre column

To drill the holes in the centre column, fit your block of wood securely on the lathe between centres. Check that it is tight enough by locking the lathe spindle and twisting the workpiece round in your hands – if

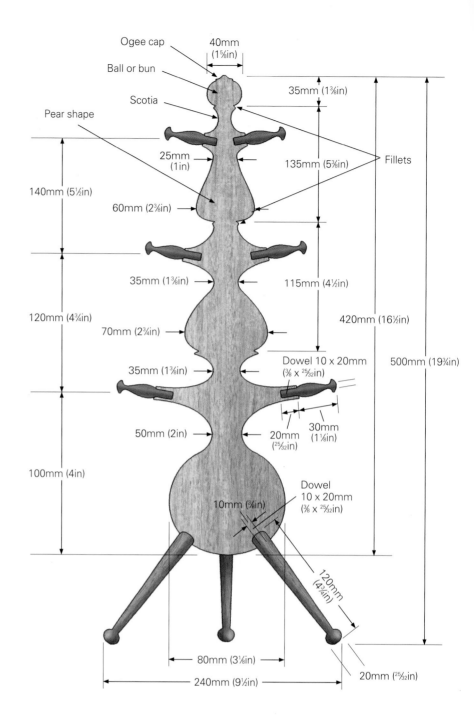

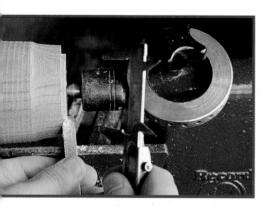

Masterchuck indexing ring ready to be screwed to a 6mm (¼in) rebate cut with a beading and parting tool at the end of the workpiece.

it turns too easily, tighten the tailstock. Set the lathe to a fairly fast speed – about 1000rpm – and turn the block to a cylinder with a sharp roughing gouge. Don't forget to wear a face mask.

If your lathe has an indexing device, move on to turning the work down to a taper, and marking out the three mug support positions around the column's circumference. I have rigged my own temporary device using a Masterchuck indexing ring.

This ring is screwed to a 6mm (¼in) rebate, cut with a beading and parting tool at the end of the workpiece. A 100mm (4in) nail acts as the arm

of the indexing jig, and a block of wood, G-cramped in a fixed position, serves as the indexing stop. A simple drilling jig completes the system, made by drilling a hole through a block of wood held in the toolrest support by a small horizontal platform.

Turn the spindle to a taper the same size as the overall dimensions of the column, using the roughing gouge. I set the toolrest at an angle to the lathe centres and use it as a straightedge. By sliding the gouge along, with my knuckles in contact with the back of the toolrest, I can create the required flatness. Mark out the vertical positions of the mug branches in a series of pencil rings. To drill the holes, the face of the drilling jig is butted up against the side of the workpiece so that the angle of all the mug supports will be the same.

The real turning

The holes for the tripod legs are drilled using the same jig, but with a larger drill size so that thicker, stronger dowels can be used for the legs.

Now the functional side of the project has been completed, you can put the drilling jig out of the way and think about the real turning. This design may look a little complex, but however many mouldings there are in such a project, they can usually be broken down into a series of hollows, rounds and steps.

Before starting on the main shapes of the column, the areas around the holes must be formed into flat surfaces onto which the mug supports can be squarely seated. Use your freshly sharpened gouge on its side, with the bevel in line with the intended cut, and slice across the mouth of the holes. With the lathe stopped, place a drill into the holes and by using it as a visual guide you can check that the angle of the cut is square with the line of the hole.

Cutting hollows

Start at the top of the column and form the hollows on each side of the top row of holes, leaving 3mm (⅛in) of flat above and below the holes. Use the

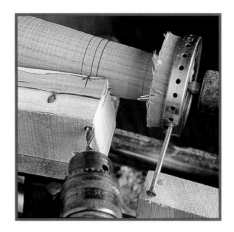

To drill the holes for the mug branches, the face of the drilling jig is butted up against the side of the workpiece, so the angle of the mug supports will all be the same.

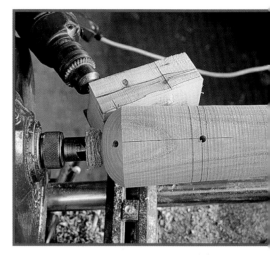

The jig is also used to drill the holes for the tripod legs, but a bigger drill bit is used.

LEFT **Using a freshly ground gouge on its side, with its bevel in line with the intended cut, slice across the mouth of the holes.**

RIGHT **You can check that the angle of cut is square with the line of the hole by placing a drill into the holes and using it as a visual guide.**

Cutting a hollow. Note the improvised vertical toolrest, made from a masonry nail.

gouge on its side and engage the cutting edge, while holding the tool firmly down on the toolrest.

Lift the handle to start the cut and as you cut, twist the tool round so it pans out at the bottom of the hollow. Repeat this on the opposite side of the hollow, using the tool in mirror fashion.

I've used an improvised vertical toolrest, made from a masonry nail fixed into a hole drilled into the top of the toolrest. By resting the back of the gouge against this support, I can avoid the tool's tendency to slip backwards at the start of the cut.

The beading and parting tool is rolled to cut a round, so the corner of the tool turns over the fibres of the wood as it twists.

Precise judgement is needed so the cut is thin enough that the waste material fractures through its end grain and falls lightly away.

Once the cut has been established, a freshly sharpened gouge will slice a clean path through the end fibres, with its bevel gliding over the surface already cut.

As you near the bottom of a deep hollow you will need to compensate for the gouge having to reach further away from the support of the toolrest, by reducing the size of cut. Once the small radius of the neck of the pear shape has been formed, you can start making the bulbous base shape.

Cutting rounds

Use the 6mm (¼in) bowl gouge to form most of the round shape – after all, its main use is for turning the outside curve of a bowl. But it will not get into the right-angle corner where the round intersects the step or fillet.

Some turners use a skew chisel for this, but it has a well-founded reputation for digging in. Cutting

small convex shapes such as balls and beads is never easy, but I find the most reliable tool for this job is the beading and parting tool.

It is used by laying the tool flat on the toolrest with the corner positioned on the crown of the round to be cut. The handle is lifted so that just the corner of the cutting edge engages with the work and lifts a tiny tuft of wood up at first. The tool is rolled so that its corner turns over the fibres of the wood as it twists.

If this is new to you, practice taking very fine cuts until you gain confidence. The point where the base of the pear shape or ball meets the surface of the fillet needs special care. At this point the beading and parting tool is almost completely on its side, and any lateral movement of the tool's edge will leave it vulnerable to snagging in the side wall of the ball. Precise judgement is needed for a cut so thin at this point that the waste material fractures through its end-grain section and falls lightly away under the pressure of the tool.

Cutting steps

The column fillets are made mainly with the beading and parting tool in the flat position on the toolrest. By lifting the handle slowly and bringing the cutting edge of the tool to bear, waste is removed in a straightforward parting cut.

Sometimes the finish benefits by removing a fine flake or two with the extreme corner of the tool's edge, using a lateral movement of the tool.

Three legs

To cut the three legs, first turn the work to a cylinder with the roughing-down gouge and cut away an area at the top of the leg where the dowel will be made, using the beading and parting tool. Part off at the base of the leg and then part down through the spindle above the ball foot, leaving a square section.

Using the beading and parting tool, cut the section into a ball. Form a taper out of the rest of the spindle using the roughing-down gouge, and round the top shoulder with the beading and

parting tool. After reducing the dowel to the correct diameter so it will fit into the base of the mug-tree column, sand and apply a coat of polish. Parting off the work at the base of the ball is done with the beading and parting tool by holding it on its side, and continuing the round, slice-cutting technique all the way round, until the spindle comes off in your hand.

To make the other two legs I find a pair of odd-leg callipers a quick and much more accurate way of transferring the lateral positions than the method of projecting a line across with a ruler and pencil.

Follow the same methods for the nine mug-tree branches as for the tripod legs, reducing the blocks to cylinders and forming dowels at the ends. The small radius at the neck of the branch is formed with a 10mm (⅜in) spindle gouge, used in the same way as the 6mm (¼in) bowl gouge, but

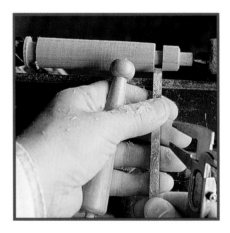

Part through the spindle above the ball foot, leaving a square section.

Taper the rest of the spindle with a roughing gouge.

Using odd-leg callipers is a quick and accurate way of transferring the lateral positions to a new leg.

Use a 10mm (⅜in) 'lady's-finger' spindle gouge to form the small radius at the neck of the branch.

more suitable for producing tight hollows because of its longer, lady's-fingernail shape. To form this long nose on the tool it has to be ground with a longer, more acute, 30° bevel.

The combination of these two things enables the tool to cut cleanly on steep concave or convex curves, but has the disadvantage of making the tool unstable to use and liable to dig in at the slightest lack of concentration.

I return to my small bowl gouge, with its less pointed cutting edge, when flattening off minor bumps and unevenness on the shallower slopes of the spindle's pear shape.

The spindle gouge comes into its own again when it comes to shaping the end of the branch, as it can form the dome shape and slice the finished work off cleanly in the same operation.

I have used seasoned elm for my mug rack, as it suits the country farmhouse style popular in the kitchens or informal dining rooms of homes today. This wood can be quite coarse in texture, but with care and sharp tools will take fairly crisp detail.

The last jobs

Start sanding with coarse abrasive to remove the last traces of tool marks, which may include quite heavy gouge ripples on the shallower slopes of the work. But they can be removed in a second or two with fresh abrasive.

The areas in deep hollows and on the steep sides of balls and pear shapes are a different story. The cleanness of these

surfaces depends on whether they have been sliced cleanly with the tools in the first place.

It's untrue to say that no amount of sanding will remedy such faults as side gashes, torn grain or uneven radiuses, but heavy sanding on these end-grain areas is almost as likely to cause added faults such as friction splits, especially if the abrasive is allowed to go blunt.

I use aluminium oxide abrasive, resin-bonded to a flexible cloth backing. I start with 80-grit and follow with 240, which removes the scratches of the coarser abrasive. I avoid sanding the fillets until the finer abrasive stage, so the crispness of the fine detail is preserved.

I sometimes roll the abrasive around a piece of dowel or convenient-sized tool handle, to get into tight radiuses, and use small sanding blocks to clean up the surface of the fillets. With elm, you can almost polish after the 240-grit, but I usually lightly rub the work with 350 or 400-grit to be certain of getting a finish where the only mark visible is the wood's grain.

Because the mug is used in kitchens and will probably come into contact with water, I've used a cellulose sealer to finish the mug tree. This is best brushed on quickly with a paintbrush, using a sheet of hardboard to protect the lathe bed from any splashes and drops.

Before it dries, wipe the work surface with a clean cotton cloth, to remove surplus polish and leave a completely even coat. This avoids the

A small bowl gouge is useful for flattening minor bumps and unevenness on the shallower slopes of the spindle's pear shape.

overlapping which can occur when polish is applied with a cloth or rubber only, and can be repeated to create any thickness of finish.

When finishing elm, I've found the surface can look disappointingly uneven immediately after the sealer has been applied. I attribute this to the unevenness in the absorbency of different areas of the grain. This defect later disappears, and the next day, when the sealer has dried, you are left with a durable and completely satisfactory finish. ■

The Shaker pegs and rail.

Shaker peg

For your first attempt at off-centre turning, try a Shaker-style peg rail

Some of the larger off-centre turning projects, such as raked chair backs and traditional Georgian turned pad feet, can be daunting for woodturners who have not done off-centre turning before.

Making a small Shaker-style peg rail gives a less formidable introduction to this useful and practical technique, which is quite easy to perform, and needs the minimum of chucking devices.

The Shaker peg rail that was the basis for this design provided a facility not just for clothes, but for chairs, candle containers, anything which needed to be stored out of the way.

The only difference in design between this rail and the traditional Shaker version is that the pegs on this rail are turned so they slope upwards. This is a better shape to hang clothes on.

One of the traditional woods used by the Shakers was cherry, but I have used English oak. There is no reason why you shouldn't use any suitable wood, from exotic rosewood

Photo 1

The three stages of peg making, starting from the top.

Photo 2

Check the diameter with vernier callipers.

to the humble pine, depending on the decor of the room the rail will be hung in. There are three main stages in making the peg (photo 1). I brought all the pegs up to the same stage before going on to the next. The top peg shows the first stage. It was turned between centres, has a tapered stem with a rounded base, and an unfinished knob at the top.

The central peg shows the work having been turned off-centre on the chuck. It was then re-centred on the lathe in the standard way, for the final turning and finishing stage.

To start

Begin by cutting the peg to the overall proportions, using a roughing gouge to remove the bulk of the waste. Cut the shoulder with a beading and parting tool.

Use vernier callipers to check the diameters are the same on each of the six pegs (photo 2). Taper the piece with a skew chisel, working the tool from the large diameter down to the narrower end (photo 3).

The off-centre jig is made from a 20 x 120mm dia disc (¾ x 4¾in). Drill a hole in the jig about 40mm (6⅝in) from the centre. I drilled the hole at right angles to the face of the plate, allowing the free end of the peg to be tensioned when pulled to the centre, adding to the strength of grip.

Fit a 25mm (1in) retaining screw through the rim to stop the peg twisting. I like to make a recess in the back of my wooden chucks and home-made accessories, so I can re-centre them for another project at a later date.

Positive hold

Hold the peg in the off-centre jig (photo 4). The knob is still cylinder-shaped, to make a more positive hold in the hole. Also, a finished knob would get damaged by the fixing screw which holds the peg in place.

The jig holds the peg at an angle while the base and dowel are turned. I use a pair of odd-leg callipers to mark the point where the base is to be cut away for a dowel (photo 5).

Photo 3

Tapering with a skew chisel, working down to the narrow end.

Photo 4

Holding the peg in the off-centre jig.

Photo 5

Marking with odd-leg callipers where the base is to be cut away.

Photo 6

Trim away the waste with a small 6mm
(¼in) bowl gouge.

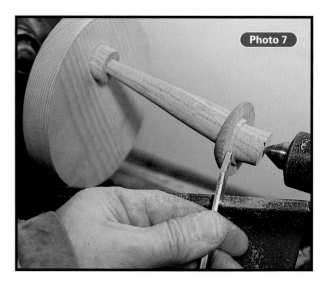

Photo 7

Reduce the dowel to a convenient diameter.

Photo 8

Round the knob with the beading and parting tool.

Photo 9

Part off with a skew chisel.

Strengthen the line with a pencil,
and trim away the waste with a 6mm
(¼in) bowl gouge (photo 6). This
puts less strain on the work than a
parting tool, which tends to become
trapped in the groove if the peg
twists slightly in the chuck.

Final stage

With the parting tool, trim square
the little bit left in the corner, and
reduce the whole dowel to a
convenient drill diameter (photo 7). It
is now time to move to the final stage.

To finish, put the work back on its
original centres, turn away the screw
hole, round the knob with the beading
and parting tool (photo 8), and apply
some suitable polish. Part off with the
skew chisel (photo 9).

Mount the pegs at regular intervals
along the rail and instal in a suitable
location. ■

Here's another attractive
project for beginners
to get cracking on:
an hour-glass in walnut

Make-up time

This hour-glass is made from English walnut, a timber which can be uninteresting in its straight-grained form, but spectacular as a burr or when taken from the base of the tree or the junction of a branch. Then, it can be wonderfully deep in tone and rich in colour.

But attractively figured wood is often difficult to work, needing care and patience and the use of much sharper tools than straight-grained wood. It's worth the time and effort, though, as figured walnut has a quality equal to many exotic hardwoods and – with the right finish – will improve with age.

Balusters

The first thing to do is prepare each of the baluster sections so they can be fitted straight onto the lathe, without having to take the drive centre out of the lathe's headstock.

Find the centres of each of the five lengths by drawing a line from corner to corner, or if you want to be more accurate, scribe four parallel lines from the sides with a cabinetmakers' marking gauge. Using a copper hammer, so that you don't damage the end of the drive centre, hammer it into the centre of each of the lengths so it forms a shallow indentation.

Grind a fresh, sharp edge on your roughing-down gouge and turn the

work to a 19mm (¾in) diameter cylinder. Put the toolrest as close as possible to the wood and set the lathe's speed to about 2000rpm.

You must wear eye protection, because with spindle turning you have to look directly into the line of the shavings and splinters as they fly off. In this case, where the spindles have short grain running diagonally across and could easily fracture, precautions are even more essential.

Before turning your spindle to the final diameter, stop the lathe and

Walnut hour-glass.

Tools needed:

19mm (¾in) roughing gouge
13mm (½in) skew chisel
6mm (¼in) beading/parting tool
6mm (¼in) bowl gouge
38mm (1½in) round-nosed
  scraper
Parting tools: one standard
  3mm (⅛in), one thin-bladed
Vernier and odd-leg callipers
Compasses
Faceplate
13mm (½in) screw chuck
10mm (⅜in) twist drill
Three-jaw Jacobs chuck
Double-sided carpet tape.

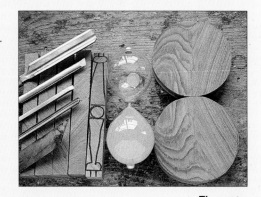

The parts.

Timbers list:

Two discs of walnut 140 x 19mm (5½ x ¾in)
Five lengths of 215 x 30 x 30mm (8½ x 1⅛ x 1⅛in)

Use callipers to check the diameter.

Odd-leg callipers are useful for transferring dimensions accurately from one spindle to another.

examine the work surface for signs of rough, broken end-grain fibres, which often occur when cutting a cylinder of figured wood where the grain runs in all directions. If there are any, you must put a finer edge on your gouge and reduce your cut, removing just a fine flake.

When satisfied with your finish, use callipers to check the diameter. Put the toolrest parallel to the work to make a fence against which you can slide your knuckles, to get the spindle thickness the same all the way along.

Once you have your spindle to the desired thickness, move the toolrest as close as you can and adjust its height, so that when the tool rests on it, you can hold the handle comfortably by your side and also see the cutting head of the tool without bending down or standing on tiptoe. When making the first spindle, carefully measure the

height of the hour-glass mechanism, minus the two sealing bungs at each end. Transfer this measurement onto the spindle and part down with a parting tool on each side of the line to form oversized areas for the dowel joints. This will also clearly define the outer parameters of the spindle.

I use a set of three odd-leg callipers to help mark out the mouldings. They are ideal for transferring the dimensions, accurately from one spindle to another. I use one set for each reference point, so they don't need altering during the job.

Use the 13mm (½in) skew chisel to form V-cuts at the intersection lines as a preparatory stage to making the central bead. The skew chisel must be ground with a very acute angle of 20° overall.

I use a wet stone for this, because on a fast dry grindstone the tip of the tool

is easily burnt, due to the thinness of the tool's cross section, which does not allow the heat to dissipate quickly enough.

Hone the tool to a razor-sharp edge on an oil or slip stone after grinding. This treatment will need to be repeated, ideally after each baluster has been made, to maintain the needed consistency of cutting action.

Skew chisel

Use the skew chisel with the longest point of the blade resting on the toolrest and bring the tip to bear so it enters the surface of the wood at a slight angle and at a point just to one side of the line.

The rest of the cutting edge must not come into contact the work at any time or the tool may bite in and veer out of control. 'Mirror' this cut on the other side of the line and enlarge the V by taking further cuts.

At the completion of each cut, the point of the tool should intersect at the bottom of the previous cut and the waste section be removed. When working straight-grained wood, the waste will immediately be sliced away by the chisel's point, but not so with figured walnut.

Instead of the point cutting through the fibres, the grain direction causes the fibres to be split apart. When this occurs you may have to stop the lathe and cut through the band of waste, and release it by hand.

When it comes to rounding the corners of the V-cut to form the bead in the middle of the baluster, change

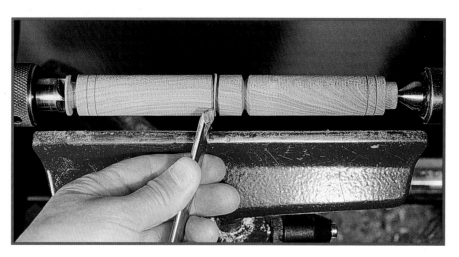

After repeating the same cut on the other side of of the line 'mirror fashion', enlarge the V by taking further cuts.

to the beading and parting tool, as it's slightly easier to handle than a skew chisel.

Place the tool at right angles to the work, with its corner resting on the crown of the bead. With the handle braced against your body, use a wrist action to twist the handle and roll the tool, so the square tip of the corner cuts away the bead's shoulder. Now form the semicircle shape of the beads.

Form the mouldings at each end of the baluster by cutting a series of square steps with the parting tool, the outer perimeters of which set the outer surfaces of the mouldings.

Parting tool

Use one of the cuts from the parting tool to set the diameter of the narrow end of the baluster's taper. Leave the widest end of the taper at the full thickness of the spindle, as it lessens the diameters that need to be measured.

As a general rule, it's best to work on the end of the spindle furthest from the drive centre first, as the workpiece near the drive centre, with its full thickness, will provide rigidity.

To form the taper, hold the skew chisel so that the cutting edge rests on the apex of the cylinder (you will probably need to raise the toolrest for this), and make sure that the edge of the tool is laid across at about 60° to the line of the spindle.

I use the tool in my right hand and steady the work with my left, having first donned a pair of thick gardening gloves to protect my palm from being burned with the the friction of the revolving work. The skew chisel handle is hugged to the lower half of my chest and my whole body moves with the cut.

It takes several passes of the tool to form the taper. Each slice must be micro-thin to prevent the work flexing on its weak, cross-grain section.

While the conventional tool for tapers is the skew chisel, you can use any cutting tool that can be brought to bear at an acute angle to the work-piece. A roughing-down gouge, when

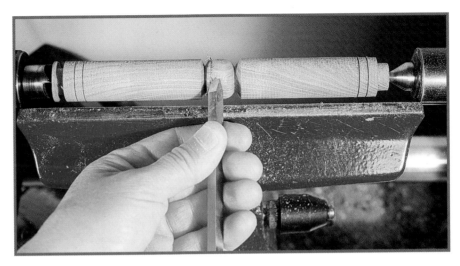

With the handle braced against your body, use a wrist action to twist and roll the tool, so the square tip of the corner cuts the shoulder of the bead and then its semi-circular shape.

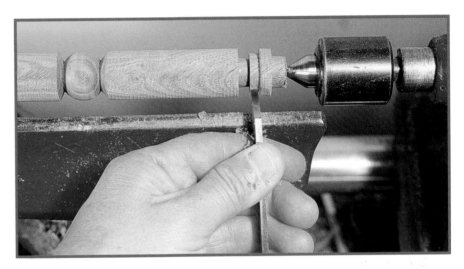

The mouldings at each end of the baluster are formed by cutting a series of square steps with the parting tool.

Use thick gardening gloves to prevent your palm from being burnt by friction from the revolving work.

Use a pencil pushed through the faceplate to centre it to the work.

The 6mm (¼in) bowl gouge is ideal for trimming the rim.

Drill a 10mm (⅜in) diameter hole in the centre of the plate.

presented to the work at a skew angle, is very efficient at removing the waste and creates a perfectly clean finish at the same time. But it works better on the near-side taper close to the headstock, where there is more support.

With both tapers completed, this leaves only the mouldings at each end of the baluster to do. Use the beading and parting tool to form the half-bead at the extreme ends of the spindle, using the same technique as for the centre bead.

Use a 6mm (¼in) bowl gouge to cut the concave shape that forms the other half of the moulding. It's used with the cutting edge on its side to start, and then twisted so the flute pans up at the completion of the cut.

Allow a small square section or fillet to remain, to form an interface between the two halves of the moulding. Finally, trim the dowels down to a regular drill size. Take care over this stage, as it will pay dividends when it come to the final assembly.

Sanding & polishing

When sanding the work, avoid running the coarser 100–250 grades of abrasive over the corners or edges of the mouldings. This will preserve crispness of detail, which can be more lightly smoothed with the finer 600-grit finishing grade. When finishing, you will find the best results come from being liberal with the abrasive. I use aluminium-oxide abrasive cloth, which lasts longer than most, but it

only works properly when it is fresh and sharp.

The best finishes for walnut are French polish, wax, or natural oils such as tung oil or walnut oil. You can use cellulose, polyurethane and plastic finishes, which are quick and easy to use and are necessary when a water- and heat-resistant surface is needed.

For a decorative effect I like to apply a coat or two of shellac French polish, using a clean cotton cloth. I buff with soft wax as soon as the shellac has dried. This polish allows the wood to oxidize with time, and gradually acquires that rich golden colour much prized by collectors of early 18th-century walnut furniture.

Hour-glass plates

Now to make the two hour-glass plates. Attach the disc to a faceplate with double-sided carpet tape. This holds the thin section firmly in place and does not leave screw holes.

I apply a piece of the tape to each surface and burnish them with a screwdriver handle. I mark the centre of the workpiece and use a pencil pushed through the faceplate to centre it onto the work. I bring the two sticky surfaces together and squeeze them in a bench vice for good measure. Using the big 38mm (1½in) round-nosed scraper makes short work of flattening the face of the disc. The tool's action is the same as for

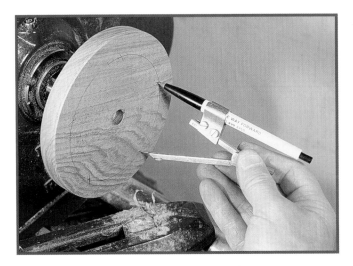

Mark the positions of the balusters by first drawing a 100mm (4in) circle onto the face of the disc with a pencil, then dividing it up with compasses spread to about 58mm (2⁵⁄₁₆in).

Reverse the plate and fit it to the screw chuck, using a wooden spacer to reduce the length of the screw.

rough-turning a spindle to a cylinder, except the scraper is held in a horizontal plane instead of the 45° cutting angle used by the gouge. The 6mm (¼in) bowl gouge is ideal for trimming the rim of the disc.

Start the cut from one corner of this and work the tool across, with the bevel of the gouge in line with the direction of the cut. Stop half-way across to avoid fraying the corners, and work in reverse.

Positions

Mark the positions of the five balusters by first pencilling a 100mm (4in) circle onto the face of the disc and then dividing it up with compasses spread to about 58mm (2⁵⁄₁₆in). Prick each point with a bradawl.

Drill a 10mm (⅜in) diameter hole in the centre of the plate, using the drill fitted into the tailstock. Wrap coloured tape around the drill to serve as a depth gauge, so you can make the hole as deep as possible without going through the plate.

This hole will be used later to hold the work on the lathe by means of a 13mm (½in) screw chuck, and it also houses the foot of the glass mechanism so the glass sits flush with the surface of the plate. Use a sanding block to flatten the surface of the plate. Once it's smooth and free of tool or coarse abrasive marks (except

for the points made by the bradawl, of course), it can be polished.

Reverse the plate and fit it onto the screw chuck, using a wooden spacer to reduce the length of the screw. Flatten the top surface of the plate and add some decoration with the corner of the beading and parting tool to form the rim of the plate.

After sanding and polishing, remove the plate from the screw chuck and drill the holes for the balusters. I used my lathe as a drill press by mounting a back plate on the tailstock and fitting a drill into the headstock.

By holding the plate against this back plate and offering it to the revolving drill, I made the upright holes for each of the balusters.

To assemble, apply a drop of glue to each dowel and gently ease the spindles into their holes. Place a heavy object on top to keep things in place while the glue dries. ■

The hour-glass made from a lighter-coloured wood.

Here's how to make a wine-bottle stand from cocobolo, which should impress your dinner guests

The completed wine-bottle stand.

Vintage stuff

Whether a candlelight dinner for two, or an informal meal with friends, a wine-bottle stand in cocobolo will enrich the occasion. The wood's beautiful colours, which range from dark burgundy to light gold, are a perfect complement to any bottle of red wine, while the close grain makes it ideal for decorative detail.

To start, you will need a wooden disc measuring 135 x 35mm (5¼ x 1⅜in), for the base and rail. Fix this on the lathe in a way that does not create screw holes in the work. I've used the hot-glue method, which involves screwing a waste scrap of pine to the

ABOVE: **Hot glue is used to make a seam between a waste scrap of pine and the faceplate. The work is attached to this.**

RIGHT: **Check that the disc is concentric, with the lathe stopped.**

faceplate and centring the workpiece on this.

Run hot glue all around to form a seam between the two and, when the glue has cooled, screw the faceplate to the lathe.

Set a speed of about 2000rpm and trim the disc's outer edge true, using a small 6mm (¼in) bowl gouge. To make the edge concentric, work the gouge from each side of the disc to the middle, so the corners don't break off.

Line up the bevel with the cut and apply only enough pressure to hold the tool in place, then feed it across so that it slices through the surface, removing a thin section of wood in one steady, controlled movement.

Concentric

Stop the lathe after each cut to check the disc is concentric and that there are no flats or saw marks left on the rim. Don't cut off more than you need – cocobolo is too precious to waste.

Flatten the face of the disc next, using a round scraper or a large bowl gouge, but the latter must not used with too heavy a cut. Use the same cutting technique as you would to turn a spindle into a parallel. Hold the gouge at a cutting angle of about 45° from the horizontal and roughly at right angles to the face of the work, then feed the tool along. Sliding the knuckle of your forefinger against the back of the toolrest will help guide the cut.

When the disc is flat and concentric, make the rail 9mm wide by 8mm deep (¹¹⁄₃₂ x ⁵⁄₁₆in) by making cuts in the face of the disc. Use a 6mm (¼in) beading and parting tool to cut a rebate about 6mm wide at the corner of the disc, and cut a groove 8mm (⁵⁄₁₆in) deep in its face, leaving the rail section between.

To mark out the balustrade, lightly scratch a centre line around the underside of the rail by holding a point against the rotating work. Now for the technical bit. You need to divide the underside of the rail into as many equal divisions as you want balusters, in this case 12. If you don't have a dividing head on your lathe, there are other methods of doing this. One is simply to use a pair of compasses or dividers.

My method is to use an indexing ring which normally fits on the back of my Masterchuck, but in this case is mounted directly to the workpiece. I carefully reduce the centre area of the work to form a short mandrel onto which to screw the index ring, using its inside thread. I G-clamp into position a wooden plate, cut to fit around the lower half of the ring, to form a stop and a marking-off point.

To operate the jig, I place a twist drill, the same size as the holes in the indexing ring, in each alternate hole. I rotate the work so that the side of the drill comes to rest on one side of the plate, and mark the position of each baluster, using the opposite position on the plate. Prick out the positions

Using a 6mm (¼in) parting tool to cut a groove about 8mm (⁵⁄₁₆in) wide.

with a fine-pointed bradawl, so the points will survive the next stage of sanding and polishing.

Whatever sealant or polish you use, you cannot wax-polish at this stage or you won't be able to get the work to grip onto the jam chuck, the next stage after parting off.

Because, when parting off the rail, you will be cutting directly into end grain, which is very hard, make sure your standard 3mm (⅛in) parting tool is extra-sharp by honing the edge on an oilstone.

Stop the lathe occasionally to monitor the cut's progress. As you

Operating the jig for marking out the balustrade.

A simple parting-cut technique is used to shape the small round moulding on the top of the rail.

approach the cutting-off point, remove the last remnant, holding the parting tool in one hand and cradling the rail in the other as it comes away.

To finish the top of the rail, press it into a shallow groove cut into a disc of scrap wood, which is then mounted on the lathe with a faceplate. Cut the groove with a 6mm (¼in) beading and parting tool, so the rail fits tightly in compression into the *outside* edge of the groove, rather than being held as on a mandrel, which might cause it to break across its short grain.

Ensure that the sides of the groove are parallel, and don't think, as some beginners do, that a taper fit will work. Making the groove the correct size is a matter of trial and error – without the error.

To make the mouldings around the edge of the wine stand, cut a series of steps with the beading and parting tool.

The hollow is then formed by cutting away the middle step with the 6mm (¼in) spindle gouge.

Checking the bottom of the base for flatness.

Using an old cheese knife to prise the stand out of the jam chuck.

Use a fresh-ground beading and parting tool to make the small round moulding on the top of the rail. First, cut two small rebates to each corner of the rail, then round off the square section between to form a capital 'D' shape.

Using a simple parting-cut technique to do the shaping, cut directly into the work at a 45° to the horizontal, always holding the edge of the tool flat. No rolling techniques or holding the tool on its side, as in spindle turning, will work here – for a crisp, clean cut you rely entirely on the sharpness of the tool edge.

After sanding and sealing, burnish in a little wax with a soft cloth until the full colour of the wood gleams

through. You can usually prise the ring out of the jam chuck with your fingers, but if you can't, cut away some of the jam chuck next to the work to free the rail.

The baluster positions on the base of the stand are marked out next. Form a flat area on the base corresponding to the underside of the rail, using the beading and parting tool. Best results are achieved by drawing the tool across the work surface in a lateral movement, with just the corner of the chisel cutting.

Mark a circle of the same diameter as the one on the underside of the rail, and fit the indexing plate in position. Mark and prick out the baluster positions as before, remove the

The lathe converted into a drill press for drilling the baluster holes in the rail and base.

Turning the balusters to a cylinder with the 6mm (¼in) bowl gouge, and marking out the central bead position with odd-leg callipers.

indexing ring and jig, and cut away the redundant mandrel.

The base of my stand has a low step which mirrors the coaster rail above, and provides a plinth on which the balusters sit. To make this feature, simply remove the waste to each side with the beading and parting tool.

Re-flatten the floor of the stand, and decorate with beads or reeds. These are scraped into the surface with a beading scraper. To make this scraper you need an 8 x 4mm (⁵⁄₁₆ x ⁵⁄₃₂in) section of high-speed steel. Using a diamond dresser, I made a round profile on a 10mm (⅜in) wide carborundum-stone wheel, to grind the shape in the end of the high-speed-steel bar.

Back to the holder

But back to the wine-bottle holder. One advantage of using a tight-grained wood like cocobolo is that it scrapes nearly as cleanly as it cuts. Bring the toolrest as close as possible to the work surface and scrape into the work with the point of the tool pointing slightly downward, to minimise the chance of the tool digging in. Use a few light cuts, and as the waste is removed from the end of the tool each time, check your progress.

Each bead is complete when the flat surface at the crown has been rounded. This ensures the beads are all the same size and that the floor of the stand stays flat.

To make the mouldings around the edge of the stand, cut a series of steps with the beading and parting tool, using a parting-cut technique. The concave or cavetto is formed by cutting away the middle step with a 6mm (¼in) spindle gouge. Hold the gouge at the standard cutting angle to the work, using only the point of the tool. Keep this at right angles to the point of cut at all times.

To sand the work, start with a fairly fine abrasive, about 240-grade aluminium oxide, followed by 400-grit. Cocobolo is an oily wood to sand and tends to clog the abrasive fairly quickly, so use plenty of abrasive. Cut it into small pieces and fold into three, so you can work the stiffened edges into the corners of the mouldings without losing the crispness of detail.

I've used French polish to seal the wood, wiped on with a clean cotton cloth. Don't apply wax at this stage, as this will prevent it from gripping in the jam chuck for the next stage.

The work is ready to be removed from its backing plate by cutting through the hot glue with a knife. I used the outer edge of the coaster's plinth as a convenient parallel surface to press into a jam chuck. I made the recess a little too wide, and needed to use a sheet of tissue paper to pack it out.

With the base firmly pressed into its recess, turn the bottom smooth with the roughing-down gouge and check the surface for flatness with a straight-edge. You can decorate the underside of the stand and even sand and polish it to the same standard as the top if you like. Alternatively, you can do as I've done and simply apply a coat or two of sealer, leaving the surface to be covered with a piece of baize.

Remove the stand from the jam chuck, using the side of an old knife to prise it out if the grip is too tight. You can drill the 5mm (³⁄₁₆in) holes for the balustrade in the rail and base of the stand, by converting your lathe into a drill press. Fit a drill in the headstock end and hold the workpiece against the back plate. Wind the tailstock so that each hole is drilled in turn. Use a piece of tape to make sure you don't drill too deep or, better still, lock your toolrest in position to act as a drill stop.

Balusters

Make the balusters separately from 10 x 10 x 35mm (³⁄₈ x ³⁄₈ x 1³⁄₈in) blanks, held on the lathe with a hollow-taper cone chuck. This most simple of wooden chucks has a taper cut into its end, which holds the square corners of the blank centrally and securely, once pressure has been applied from the opposite end by the tailstock centre.

This is not just a quick means of mounting the work on and off the lathe, but also positions small pieces like these balusters where they are more easily accessible to the tools.

Bring a small toolrest as close as you can, and turn the work to an 8mm (⁵⁄₁₆in) cylinder using a 6mm (¼in) bowl gouge. With a 3mm (⅛in) parting tool, cut the work to length by forming two dowel sections at each end.

You have now formed the overall perimeters of the balustrade. Use odd-leg callipers to mark out the position of the central bead. Cut this with the bead scraper. Make the two adjacent beads in the same way and taper the remaining outer sections with a 13mm (½in) skew chisel. Start the cut on the apex of the cylinder, so the tool can nestle comfortably against your body. To copy the balusters, I set up

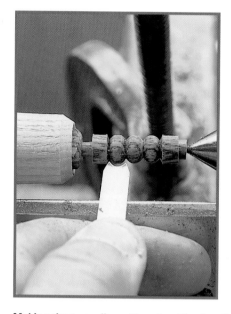

Making the two adjacent beads with a beading scraper and tapering the remaining outer sections with a 13mm (½in) skew chisel.

two or three callipers to do the necessary dimensions, so I need not re-set them for each spindle.

Assemble the wine stand by using a drop of slow-setting epoxy glue to the ends of each baluster and weighting the rail down with a heavy book. When this has dried, apply and trim the baize. Wipe a clean piece of abrasive across the sharp edge of the base to cut it and remove the waste. This makes a very neat job and will protect polished surfaces. ■

Trimming the green baize with clean abrasive.

The completed wine stand.

The completed mirror.

Mirror this

This attractive hand mirror in pear and violet rosewood shows what a difference the choice of wood can make to the success of the finished article

Timber selection is as important as attention to fine detail to a decorative object, especially if you are combining different woods in one project. Finding complementary timbers is an art in itself.

Even when the feature is as tiny as the astragal ring on this hand-mirror frame, the colour and texture of the wood must be carefully chosen. I thought the deep purple colour of the violet rosewood would bring out the rosiness of the European pear used for the frame and handle.

The pinkness of the pear was caused by steam treatment before it was air seasoned. Many fine-textured woods are suitable for mirror frames, provided they are well seasoned and stable. Any major shrinkage or warping after assembly and it is likely to split the mirror in two or crack the glass.

Astragal ring

As well as forming a decorative border, the astragal ring hides the gap between the outside rim of the mirror and the inside edge of the frame. Making the ring first makes it much easier to produce an accurate fitting for it in the body of the frame.

The total width of the astragal section is only 3mm (⅛in), so there is no room for error when cutting it to size. The inside diameter should overlap the edge of the mirror plate by about 1mm (³⁄₆₄in).

Leave a millimetre gap around the edge of the plate to allow for any shrinkage in the frame. This leaves the last millimetre to overlap the inside edge of the frame.

Seeing clearly can be difficult when making these tiny details, especially in dark timber, so it may help to work in a strong light.

I made my astragal ring out of the outside edge of a small bowl blank, an area usually cut away to form the outside curve of the bowl. By doing this I made use of an area of wood which would otherwise be wasted.

I use double-sided tape to hold the disc onto a faceplate, so I don't compromise the usefulness of the disc

Add 6mm (¼in) to your callipers and form the outside rim of the moulding.

Make a 1mm (³⁄₆₄in) step in the inside
edge of the astragal.

Round off the outer square section by
first making simple parting cuts.

Using a thinner parting tool will give you
more control.

Part off the ring by cutting through the
back with a thin parting tool.

with screw holes. I burnish the tape
down to both surfaces with the handle
of a screwdriver before bringing the
two surfaces together and squeezing
them in the bench vice.

Set a lathe speed of about 1000rpm
and mount the disc on the lathe with
the toolrest adjusted just below centre
height, and as close as possible to the
workface.

Smooth off an area at the edge of the
disc's face with a 10mm (³⁄₈in) beading
and parting tool, using normal parting-
cut technique, with the handle at about
45° to the horizontal.

Measure the mirror plate's diameter
with vernier callipers, reduce this
measurement by 2mm (³⁄₆₄in) and cut
into the face of the rosewood disc to
form the inside edge of the astragal.

A thin 3mm (¹⁄₈in) parting tool is best
for this job, but hone the edge on an
oilstone so it will cut cleanly. With a

wood like violet rosewood you can
achieve fine, crisp detail without much
trouble, as long as the tools are kept
sharp.

Add 6mm (¼in) to your callipers and
form the outside perimeter of the
moulding by making another parting
cut 4mm (⁵⁄₃₂in) deep. Then form a
1mm (³⁄₆₄in) step in the inside edge of
the astragal and round the outer square
section by first making simple parting
cuts with the parting tool at about 45°
to the workface.

Move the tool rest round to the outer
edge of the disc and make the undercut
at the back of the astragal. This is 1mm
x 1mm (³⁄₆₄ x ³⁄₆₄in) and forms the small
overlap which hides the inside corner
of the mirror frame.

Be ultra-careful when making this
rebate, because you are cutting directly
into the end fibres of the disc, which
are much harder when cut head-on
than from the side. For better control,
use a thin parting tool, which reduces
the width of cut.

Final round shape

The final round shape of the astragal
moulding is done with abrasive. You
need not use very coarse abrasive – 240-
grit aluminium oxide to start, followed
by 400 or 600 to finish off. By tightly
folding the abrasive, you can work into
the corners of the mouldings, without
rounding the square corners.

Apply shellac pale polish, wiped on
so it runs into the crevices, followed by
pure carnauba wax, rubbed on with

the lathe running. Burnish with a soft
cotton cloth for a bright finish.

Part off the ring by cutting through
the back with the thin parting tool held
in your left hand, and the astragal
should fall lightly into your other hand.

If this parting off method seems
incautious after all this patient work,
you could provide a cardboard box
with a soft lining for the ring to fall
into. This leaves both hands free to
hold the parting tool.

The main frame

I made the mirror frame from the
front 20mm (¾in) of a bowl blank,
mounted on the lathe as before, using
double-sided tape. Carefully measure
the mirror plate with the vernier
callipers and add 2mm (³⁄₆₄in). Mark
this on the disc.

Reduce the outside of the disc to the mirror
frame width by slicing though the edge of
a bowl blank with a 6mm (¼in) bowl gouge.

A square-cornered scraper is needed for hollowing the square corners and trimming the recess to its final size.

Using a beading and parting tool to form a small outer bead on the corner.

Parting off the frame section with an extra-long-handled parting tool.

RIGHT **A mandrel is used to hold the frame on the lathe so that the back of the frame can be worked.**

A 16mm (²⁴⁄₃₂in) wide frame is enough to support the weight of the mirror plate and to receive the handle dowel. Reduce the outside of the disc to the desired mirror frame width by slicing through the edge of the bowl blank with a small 6mm (¼in) bowl gouge.

By feeding the tool from the side with the gouge's bevel in line with the cut, you can create a very smooth finish, especially on timber as evenly textured as pear.

You can also use the gouge to remove some of the bulk from the face of the disc to make the recess for the mirror plate, but you will need a square-cornered scraper for hollowing the square corners and trimming the recess to the final size.

I use a standard 32mm (1¼in) square-ended scraper, modified for hollowing square-sided cavities by having the lower edge of its left side ground away, so it doesn't interfere

with the wall or side it is cutting.

To decorate the mirror frame, I made a simple cushion with a small outer bead formed on the corner. Use a beading and parting tool to make this. Cut across the face of the frame by slightly twisting the tool and cutting with the leading corner of the tool's edge. Repeat this a few times, sweeping the material completely away from one side, but stopping short on the outer side to leave a 3–4mm (⅛–⁵⁄₃₂in) square section, for the bead.

To make this, follow the same method as for the astragal's bead. Before sanding, make sure the astragal fits comfortably into its recess and

there is enough depth to take the thickness of the mirror plate.

After sanding and polishing with shellac and carnauba wax, I parted off the frame section, using my extra-long-handled parting tool. You can stop the parting operation 25mm (1in) before the final parting off, and make the final separation with a handsaw, with the lathe switched off. But the more adventurous may like to part nearly all the way and then stop the lathe and break the last 5mm (³⁄₁₆in) by hand.

A mandrel made from a softwood disc is used to hold the frame on the lathe so the back of the frame can be worked. To make the mandrel, screw

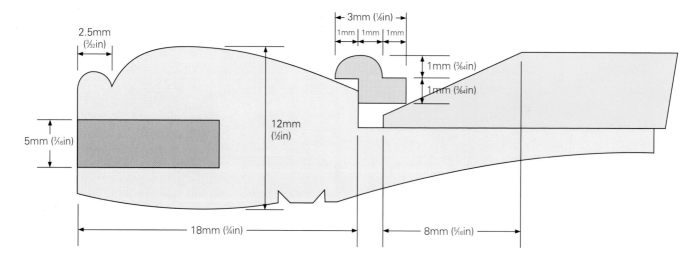

2.5mm (³⁄₃₂in)

5mm (³⁄₁₆in)

12mm (½in)

3mm (⅛in)

1mm | 1mm | 1mm

1mm (³⁄₆₄in)

1mm (³⁄₆₄in)

18mm (¾in)

8mm (⁵⁄₁₆in)

Using the bowl gouge to cut across the face and form a shallow dish.

Trimming the small button in the centre of the back with the beading and parting tool.

The decoration is completed by cutting a pair of lines close to the outer edge of the frame.

the disc to a faceplate and trim the edge parallel, so it forms a tight fit in the frame's recess.

Jam the frame onto the mandrel and make sure it runs true before you begin work. Use the bowl gouge to cut across the face and form a shallow dish, which will reduce the weight of the mirror but not its strength.

Leave a small button in the centre of the back for decoration, trimming it to shape with a beading and parting tool, using simple parting cuts.

Complete decoration

Complete the decoration with a pair of lines cut close to the outer edge of the frame, using the corner of the beading and parting tool. Drill a 5mm (³⁄₁₆in) diameter hole through the side of the frame, to hold the handle dowel, before sanding and polishing.

In the sanding stage the full beauty of the wood can be revealed. The purpose of sanding is not simply to make the

surface smooth, but to remove all tool marks, which usually can only be seen when you are applying finer grades of abrasive.

You may even find a stubborn blemish or scratch when putting on the polish. You will not be the first turner to have to start all over again with abrasive, to ensure the only marks showing are those caused by the grain.

A strong stream of dust is a sure sign that sanding is going well. Don't use your abrasive when it's blunt, as this often causes the fine end-grain cracking which can spoil a piece. The surface should always have a light chalky appearance during sanding.

Wipe the surface clean before applying shellac, with the lathe stationary. Use a clean cotton cloth with a soft full pile, which gets polish into the crevices of the fine detail.

You can build up the polish to a heavy gloss by applying more coats, but I prefer to use the carnauba wax

Drilling a 5mm (³⁄₁₆in) diameter hole through the side of the frame to hold the dowel of the mirror's handle.

Shaping the base curve of the handle with a ⅜in spindle gouge.

The ¼in bowl gouge is used to shape the bulbous end of the handle.

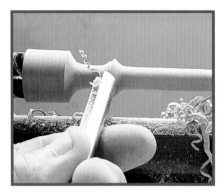

Reducing the stem, leaving enough wood to turn a bead.

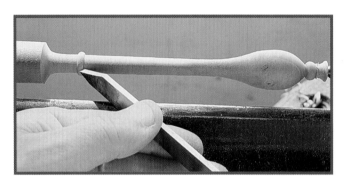

Forming the bead.

to create a bright, deep finish. After applying two or three coats of shellac, leave the polish to dry for about 10 minutes. Then rub the surface with a carnauba stick and burnish into the work, so it melts and spreads evenly. Apply the wax again, but this time burnish with much less pressure, until you get a bright sparkling finish. When satisfied, gently prise the work off the mandrel so that you don't spoil the finish.

The handle

The mirror's handle is made from pearwood 180mm long x 30mm square (7 x 1⅛in). Turn the block to a cylinder using a 19mm (¾in) roughing gouge, with the lathe set at 2000rpm.

Start shaping the handle at the revolving centre end, so the total width of the workpiece is maintained, supporting the work until completion.

A 10mm (⅜in) spindle gouge is ideal for shaping the base curve of the handle, its ladies' fingernail end being able to get into tight spaces.

Feed the gouge into the corner of the cylinder on its side, and use the point to slice through the wood, with the bevel of the tool forming the convex shape in a series of fine cuts. By using the gouge even more on its side, and alternating the direction, form the sides of a small bead at the handle's base.

For the rest of the handle shaping, use a 6mm (¼in) bowl gouge. This does not have the point of the spindle gouge and is more easy to control. It's used in the same way, with the bevel resting on the work and slicing round the top of the handle's base to make a bulbous form which fits comfortably in the hand.

Trim the stem of the handle in a series of cuts, gradually reducing it to the finished thickness before making another cut further along and gradually working back toward the drive centre end.

To make a bead at the handle's neck, leave a small area thicker than the rest and reduce the stem on the other side by cutting in the opposite direction with the gouge.

Turn this small diamond section into a bead by first reducing it to a small

square section, using the parting tool in a series of simple parting cuts and cutting the corners away with the same tool until you get the round profile.

The dowel, made with series of parting cuts, is best left until after the sanding and polishing to preserve the strength at the drive end of the work.

The handle's final parting off is done with a skew chisel, by slicing through the narrow section of wood on the other side of the ball at the base of the handle.

All that remains is to assemble the mirror's parts and glue them together with strong epoxy. I used the mandrel with a weight on top to hold the astragal in position while the glue set. ■

Made to order

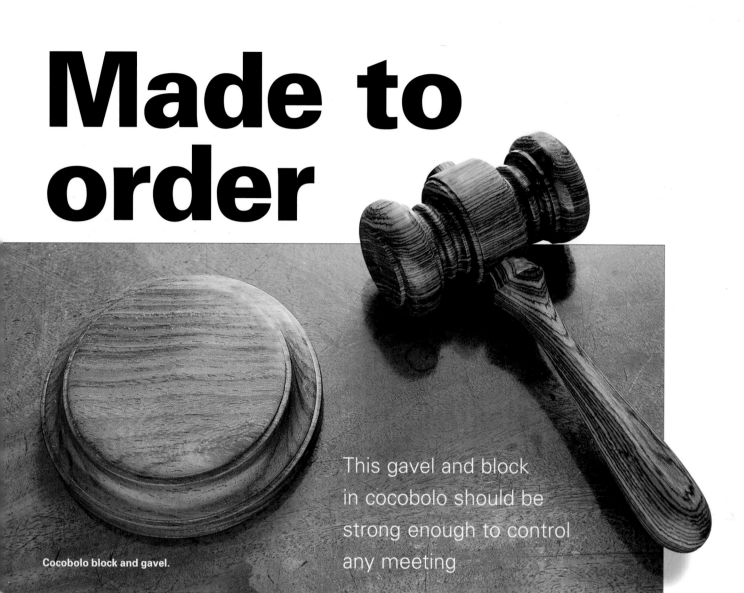

This gavel and block in cocobolo should be strong enough to control any meeting

Cocobolo block and gavel.

Tools used

The tools you will need for this project are (left to right):

19mm (¾in) roughing gouge

Standard 3mm (⅛in) parting tool

10mm (⅜in) beading and parting tool

6mm (¼in) bowl gouge

5mm spindle gouge

Beading scraper made from a 10mm (⅜in) wide scraper

Vernier callipers

Odd-leg callipers

Turning small-scale objects like this gavel and block can be just as satisfying as larger projects, especially when the wood used is as rich and colourful as cocobolo.

In some ways, fine decorative detail calls for more concentration than turning wider, more sweeping forms. For example, any attention lapse when hollowing a bowl may cause an ugly gash which can usually be cut out, but if the same thing happens to a fine bead or essential detail, you've had it!

You must be disciplined, having everything prepared and taking one step at a time. Tools must be sharp, and one or two may have to be customised for specific tasks.

If you need a chucking device to hold the work on the lathe, make it before starting the project. Have vernier and odd-leg callipers to hand, ideally several, set at different dimensions. With everything prepared in this way, work should go smoothly.

The head of the gavel is made from a block of cocobolo 55 x 55 x 110mm (2⅛ x 2⅛ x 4⅜in), and the handle from a length 30 x 30 x 200mm (1⅛ x 1⅛ x 8in). Cocobolo is ideal for gavels, being solid and having a dense, even grain which will take crisp, fine detail.

The gavel head

Make the hole for the handle at right angles through the axis of the gavel head. This is best done when the block is still square.

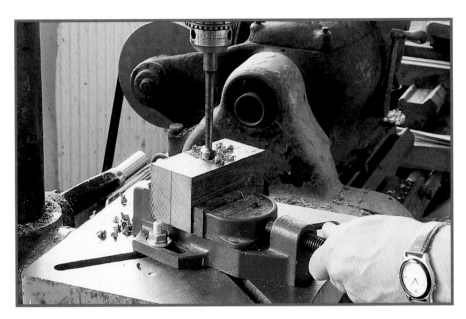

Centre-punching and drilling a 15mm (⅝in) diameter hole, using a drill press.

Check the block with a set square and plane it square if necessary before marking a centre line across each end and along one side of the block.

Centre-punch the position of the hole half way along the line and drill a 15mm (⅝in) diameter hole. It's easiest done on a drill press, especially if you have a hand vice you can bolt to the bed of the press.

Another method is to drill the hole through the block, using your lathe as a drill press. To do this, screw a disc of scrap pine or plywood to a faceplate and mount this on the lathe. Stick the block to this backing plate with double-sided carpet tape, using a saw-tooth centre secured in the tailstock to position the block. You can remove the assembly and press it more firmly together in a vice to ensure the tape grips well.

Remount the work and, with the lathe speed set to about 500rpm, wind in the tailstock so the stationary drill cuts a hole right through the revolving workpiece. Prise the block off its backing and hammer a drive centre into the centre of one end. Using a copper-headed hammer will avoid damaging the drive centre's taper.

With a timber as hard as cocobolo, the jaws of the centre will indent no more than 1mm (³⁄₆₄in) into the end-grain surface of the block. Mount the work between centres and tighten the tailstock so it's held securely. Test the tightness by locking the headstock spindle and twisting the workpiece by hand. If it revolves or becomes dislodged from its centres, it will need more turns of the tailstock hand wheel.

If the work does become dislodged, a useful precaution against losing the centre is to mark the end of the workpiece with an arrow showing the position of the drive centre's grub screw or some other reference point. This enables you to quickly relocate the work to the same drive prongs.

Adjust the toolrest so it runs parallel with the edge of the work, about 13mm (½in) below the height of the centre of the workpiece, and set the speed to about 2000rpm.

Revolve the work by hand to ensure the corners of the block don't foul the toolrest when the work rotates, and check that its levers and the tailstock barrel locks are tight before switching on the lathe.

Warning

Before you start turning, a word of warning. Drilling the hole first creates a minor safety problem, especially for turners who use their hand to check the work's roundness or to slow it down after switching off the lathe. To avoid trapping your finger in the hole, seal it with bung made from scrap wood.

Turn the work to a cylinder using a well-sharpened 19mm (¾in) roughing gouge. Use the straight edge of the

Using odd-leg callipers to get both sides of the gavel head exactly the same length.

Cutting away waste material with a razor-sharp and perfectly square 10mm (⅜in) beading/parting tool, using vernier callipers to check the dimensions are the same on each side of the gavel head.

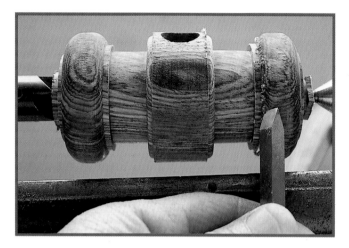

Forming the bun by rolling the tool both sides.

Feeding the tool into the work at about 90° to the horizontal, so the full shape of the bead is formed.

toolrest as a guide to run your knuckles against and test each end of the cylinder with vernier callipers to check they are the same diameter.

The curve of the gouge will cause a slightly rippled surface which can be minimised by feeding it more slowly across the work. When you are sure the cylinder is parallel, start marking out the lateral dimensions of the gavel head.

Square steps

The hole in the middle of the gavel is an excellent reference point from which to measure the ends of the finished gavel. Use odd-leg callipers to get both sides of the gavel head exactly the same length. Part down with a parting tool on the outside edge of each of these lines, to clearly define the gavel's perimeters.

Using the end surfaces of the gavel head as reference points to work from, mark out the areas on each side of the gavel head which divide the main central drum where the handle is fitted from the two bulbous bun shapes on each side of the head.

With a razor-sharp and perfectly square ⅜in (10mm) beading and parting tool, cut away the waste material, and use vernier callipers to check the dimensions are equal on each side of the gavel head.

Form two fillets, or square steps, on each side of the buns in the same way. Reducing the work to a series of square steps sets out the perimeters of each part and gives square corners

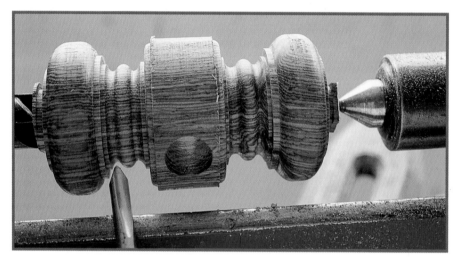

Forming the concave hollows to each side of the bead with a 5mm spindle gouge, ground with a long, round nose.

from which to take dimensions. It also reduces the whole job to a series of smaller, manageable bites.

Buns and beads

Don't start shaping until both sides of the gavel head are the same. Then lay aside your callipers and form the round bun shapes by eye, using the beading and parting tool.

Position the tool so the blade rests flat against the crown of the work with one corner of the tool in line with the centre of the bun. Twist the tool so the corner of the blade touches the surface and slightly lifts the fibres.

Continue rolling the tool to cut off the corner of the workpiece, repeating this until a half-round has been formed. Do exactly the same on the reverse side of the bun.

Form the in-and-out shape by first cutting a bead in the middle of each of the two narrow sections of the gavel head. An advantage of using dense-grained wood is that it will take fine detail, even when using a basic scraping technique.

To use a bead-forming scraper on coarse wood such as pine would end in a crumbly mess, but with cocobolo you can hardly tell whether it's been scraped or sliced. Make sure your scraper is very sharp and that, in use, the toolrest is as close as possible to the workface. Feed the tool into the work at about 90° to the horizontal, so the full shape of the bead is formed.

A 5mm (³⁄₁₆in) spindle gouge, ground with a long round nose, is used to form the concave hollows on each side of the bead. Each side of the hollow is cut

ABOVE AND LEFT
Finishing the ends of the gavel head in a collet chuck.

separately. Start at the edge with the gouge on its side, and as it slices into the work surface twist it so that the flute pans out at the floor of the hollow.

The smoothest results, when sanding, are obtained with aluminium oxide abrasive, bonded to a flexible cloth. I start with medium 240 grit, and end with 400. Wear a dust mask, to avoid breathing in cocobolo's fairly acrid dust.

I also usually wear gardening gloves when sanding, to protect my hands from being friction-burnt by the rotating work.

You can seal the work with a coat of French polish or cellulose sealer, but don't use wax or oil at this stage, or you'll be unable to grip the work well at the next.

Collet chuck

A collet chuck is ideal for holding the gavel head securely without damaging its polished waist, during turning, sanding and polishing. To make the chuck, select a block of seasoned hardwood and screw it to a faceplate.

If you want to re-use the chuck at a later date, you will need to recess the faceplate into the back of the block before securing it with the screws. Turn the 100 x 75 x 75mm (4 x 3 x 3in) block to a cylinder and flatten the face by slicing across with a gouge.

Use a slightly undersize drill, so if it wanders slightly off course you can skim the sides of the hole true with the corner of a square-nosed scraper. Taper the outside of the cylinder and leave the sides 4mm (⁵⁄₃₂in) thick at the end, before sawing the chuck along its length to form eight equal jaws.

Cut the collar from a scrap of 15mm (⁵⁄₈in) plywood, so it slides over the tapered body of the chuck and compresses it.

Press the gavel head into the collet chuck and push the collet ring on, until it squeezes the jaws tight. Slice away the waste with a parting tool, so the face of the gavel head is clean and flat.

After working one face of the gavel, loosen the collar compressing the chuck jaws to release the gavel head. This is then reversed and the opposite end finished in the same way.

A bright carnauba wax finish can now be applied. This hard wax is rubbed on with the lathe running, so that a thin coat is melted on the surface. This is burnished with soft flannelette-cotton cloth until it melts and spreads into the grain.

It is then burnished with less pressure to produce a spectacular shine.

Gavel handle

The handle is straightforward spindle turning. Turn the block to a cylinder with the roughing gouge and reduce a section at one end to a 15mm (⁵⁄₈in) dowel, using a beading and parting tool.

Form the main shape of the handle with the roughing gouge, working the tool from the high dimensions into the bottom of the shallow curves. Cut away an area near the drive centre with a standard parting tool, to make working space for a beading and parting tool.

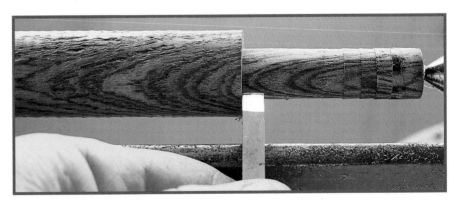

After turning the handle block to a cylinder, a section at one end is reduced to a 15mm (⁵⁄₈in) dowel with a beading and parting tool.

LEFT **Using a roughing gouge to shape the main handle.**

Forming the moulding to the edge of the block with the beading and parting tool.

The concave curves on the edge are formed with a small bowl gouge.

Cut the smaller curve at the butt end of the handle with the beading tool, following the same procedure as when making the buns for the gavel head. After sanding and polishing the handle, part off this end with the corner of the beading and parting tool, by simply continuing the beading cut.

Catch the work before it falls to the floor and use a little hand work to complete finishing.

Block or anvil

Use the double-sided tape method to mount the 120mm (4⅞in) disc on a faceplate with scrap pine between. Trim the edges true with the 6mm (¼in) bowl gouge by slicing across with the tool on its side.

Work from the front edge to the centre to start, then from the back corner, so you create a clean corner to the anvil's base edge. Flatten the face with a round-nosed scraper, used in the same way as for rough-turning a spindle to a cylinder, only the scraper is held in a horizontal plane rather than a 45° cutting angle.

Make the edge moulding with a combination of square parting cuts, using the beading and parting tool, and concave curves with the small bowl gouge.

Use a sanding block to flatten the surface, and after prising the anvil off the lathe, cover the base with green baize. ■

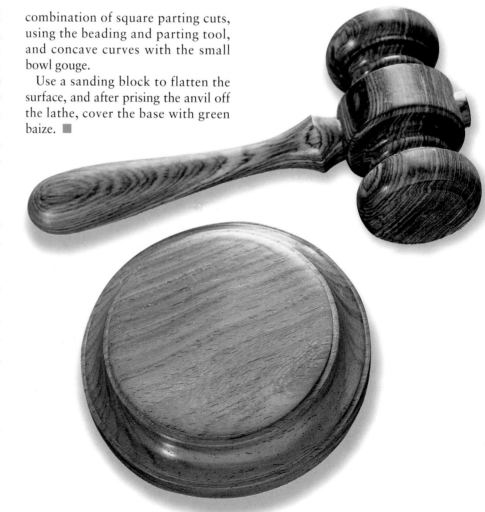

Light work

How to make a pair of mopane rosewood candlesticks, graceful enough to make any romantic dinner really special

Using the lathe to drill the hole in the base of the candlestick.

C andlelight is still preferred to electric light for special meals with friends and loved ones. So candlesticks are as popular as ever. They can be made in any style to suit the occasion and harmonise with the room decor.

There is plenty of scope for creativity, but bear in mind that to be able to reproduce one object from another, it helps to have clear datum points to copy. One reason why I use traditional designs so often is that they have clear intersection points between each shape, which can easily be transferred.

This pair of mopane rosewood candlesticks involves making a number of peardrop shapes and regular round and hollow mouldings. The overall effect may seem daunting at first, but by breaking the job down into easy steps, the problems can be more easily overcome.

The bases are made from two 150mm (6in) discs, 45mm (1¾in) thick. The stems from 45mm (1¾in) square stock 460mm (18in) long.

Drill a hole at perfect right angles through the centre of the base by applying double-sided tape to one side of your disc and mounting it on the lathe, using a faceplate fitted with a piece of backing wood.

With the lathe set at no more than 500rpm, drill the hole. The size is determined by the width of the thread on the tap between its threads. Cut right through, until you hit the backing. As a safety precaution, I stop the lathe after the hole has been made, before withdrawing the drill, in case its taper comes loose from its hold in the tailstock.

Thread cutting

This pair of candlesticks has a screw joint to hold the stem into the base, a refinement which enables the candlesticks to be dismantled and stored away in a drawer when not in use.

Cut the thread with the disc held securely in the jaws of the bench vice. I have used an old wooden screw tap (picked up at a second-hand tool stall), which I feed through the hole, rather than winding it back, as this tends to damage the wooden thread.

You can make a serviceable tap out of a very coarse-threaded bolt, by filing two deep slots laterally along the length of thread.

Making a screw chuck

I've made a wooden screw chuck to centre the disc on the lathe, which allows the work to be swopped round in an instant, giving access to each side of the workpiece in turn.

To make the chuck, mount a 100 x 100 x 63mm (4 x 4 x 2½in) block of mild-grained hardwood such as beech or sycamore on the lathe. Make sure the grain direction is running along the length of the block, so it provides the necessary strength for the threaded spigot. Turn the block to a 100mm (4in) diameter disc and cut a 25mm (1in) long spigot to the same diameter as the widest diameter of the tap.

Mark out the spiral thread with a flexible strip of plastic the same width as one of the threads on the tap, and cut the thread.

The wooden screw chuck should, if possible, be given a recess into which a faceplate can be fitted and re-centred accurately, so the chuck can be re-used at a later date.

Flatten base

With the disc secured on the screw chuck, set the speed to about 2000rpm and use a large round-nosed scraper to flatten off the bottom of the base.

After sanding smooth, turn the disc round on the chuck and face off the top of the base in the same way. Trim the edge of the disc with a 6mm (¼in) bowl gouge by slicing across the surface from each side, with the bevel of the tool in line with the cut.

With wood as hard as this, you may need to make one or two passes, re-sharpening the gouge each time.

When the disc has been made true, with square angles to the rim, you can mark it out for the base shape. I've used a traditional base shape, comprising an ogee which starts at the top of the base, near where the stem of the candlestick is joined, and flows down, ending with an upright square section or fillet. Below this, the bottom

ABOVE **Mounting the blank disc onto the lathe using the wooden screw chuck.**

LEFT **Cutting the thread in the hole of the candlestick base using a tap.**

Using a large round-nosed scraper to flatten off the disc.

Slicing the rim of the disc square and true with the 6mm (¼in) bowl gouge.

Marking out the moulding intersections using a pair of odd-leg callipers.

Cutting the V-shape at the head of the ogee with the beading and parting tool.

Forming the ogee shape of the base with a 13mm (½in) spindle gouge.

Cutting the square section for the quarter-round toe of the base.

Using the lathe to drill out the socket in the top of the candlestick stem.

rim of the base is shaped with a half-bead.

Record the dimensions before you cut away the square corners of the disc which contain the reference points of the shape, so they can be more easily copied for the twin.

Work from the front of the disc and cut a right-angled step in the corner of the disc with the 10mm (⅜in) beading and parting tool. Use the tool at about 45° to the vertical and feed it into the surface of the work, removing a section no more than a few millimetres wide at each forward stroke.

The square section formed at the bottom edge of the disc will be made into the half-bead of the base.

Angled step

Use the same tool in a lateral direction to form an angled step in the disc, about 25mm (1in) away from the edge of the centre hole. From the base of this step springs the convex curve of the ogee shape, which is formed by slightly twisting the tool so the leading corner of the edge is brought into play.

The rest of the ogee is formed with a 13mm (½in) spindle gouge, used on its side. Make sure you only engage the point, while keeping the bevel as flat against the surface of the work as possible.

Work the tool in the direction of the grain, from the centre outwards, removing very little at first, but increasing the depth of cut as you approach the outer edge. To finish off, you will probably need to re-sharpen the gouge and take very fine cuts with the tip, especially near the base of the ogee where you want to leave a crisp square upright section to form a fillet.

Hone the beading and parting tool

again before using it to form the half-bead at the edge of the base. You will have to use a parting cut technique at the base of the step or fillet but, where possible, make the curved shape of the bead by using a lateral shearing technique, with just the corner of the edge engaged.

This means working the tool slowly sideways, gyrating the handle of the tool in a short arc, while squeezing the shaft sideways between finger and thumb.

Stem

You can use the lathe again for drilling out the candle socket for the brass liner in the top of the candlestick. Mark out the centres at each end of your work. Centre-punch one end, and hammer the drive centre into the other.

Secure a saw-toothed centre or an equivalent drill bit in the headstock and place the drive centre in the tailstock. With the workpiece braced against the drive centre's prongs, and with the lathe set at no more than 500rpm, feed your workpiece into the drill by winding in the tailstock. When you have a hole about 25mm (1in) deep, switch off the lathe before withdrawing the work from the drill.

First candlestick

Use a wooden bung in the candle socket to support and re-centre the workpiece on the tailstock and turn to a cylinder with the roughing gouge.

Slice the top of the stem clean and square with the skew chisel and mark out the intersection positions of the beads and peardrop shapes which make up your overall design.

Start making the shapes at the end furthest away from the headstock,

Slicing the top of the stem clean with a skew chisel.

Forming a bead: first make small V-cuts on each of the intersection lines...

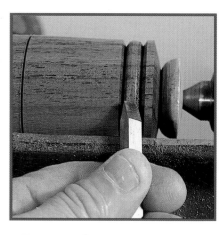

...then round off the corners and form the bead with the 10mm (⅜in) beading tool.

Using a pair of odd-leg callipers to mark out the mouldings.

Cutting down to form the outer diameter of the bead.

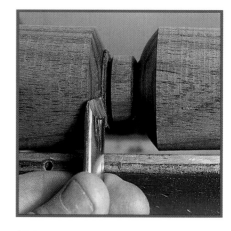

Slicing with the skew to form the V-cuts either side of the bead section.

Using a 13mm (½in) gouge to shape the waist section of the top of the stem.

Rounding the base of the waist section with the beading and parting tool.

so the full width of the workpiece is left intact, supporting the work and keeping it rigid.

Use a freshly honed skew chisel to make two shallow V-cuts on the lines at the top of the stem and form a bead by rounding off the corners with the edge of a beading and parting tool. Place the tool edge flat on the surface of the section and twist it, so the corner engages and lifts the wood fibres slightly.

Continue twisting until the corner is round, ending with the tool on its side, in the point of the V-cut. Cut one side first, and then the other, until a perfect half-round section is formed.

Making beads

Making beads requires practice. The way to avoid snatching is to make each cut so fine that no lateral force is exerted on the cut, as this could pull the tool off course.

Use the beading tool to cut away the waste between the lower pair of lines, until the diameter of a smaller bead section is formed. Slice the shoulders down with a skew chisel and form two identical V-cuts on each side of the bead section, then round off the middle section and form the bead using the same technique as before.

Make the waist shape of the stem into a gentle ogee with the 13mm (½in) bowl gouge and round off the base where it meets the small bead with the beading and parting tool.

To make the twin candlestick, the lateral dimensions of the first candlestick are transferred using odd-leg callipers. Set up the original candlestick so it can be easily referred to. The peardrop shapes are formed by first making a deep V-cut at the base of the shape and then rounding the corner with the beading tool, as if you were forming a large bead.

Use the spindle gouge to hollow the waist of the peardrop. No measurements are needed after the initial outer parameters of the shape have been formed, except, perhaps, where the thickness of the waist may need to be checked.

This saves time when it comes to relaying dimensions, but needs a good eye for judging proportions. The best guide is to always make the most perfect geometrical ball and hollow shapes you can, each time, without

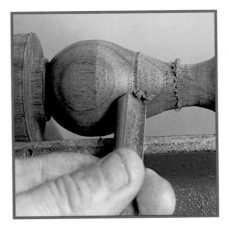

Using odd-leg callipers to transfer the lateral moulding positions.

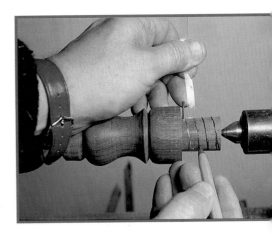

Using a 13mm (½in) spindle gouge to form the waist of the peardrop shape.

Using a vertical post to support the back of a gouge on critical cuts.

Marking out the screw threads on the dowel section of the stem.

slavishly sticking to the original.

The hollow shape in the middle of the candlestick stem is formed with a 10mm (⅜in) spindle gouge, after parting away the waste section – in the same way as you would for a small bead. Use the tool on its side to start the cut, and twist it round as the cut proceeds, so it pans out at the bottom of the hollow.

This is repeated on each side until the depth of the hollow is reached. To prevent the tool slipping at the beginning of its cut, I have provided a small vertical tool post, made out of a masonry nail, placed in a hole in the toolrest, on which the back of the tool can be pivoted. This makes it much easier to preserve the corners of the two thin square sections or fillets, which are often used to articulate between curved mouldings.

Threaded dowel

Make a dowel on the bottom end of the candlestick stem, the same diameter as the tap. To ensure the shoulder is cut clean, cut through the surface fibres with the point of the skew chisel first, then part down with the beading and parting tool.

Position one end of the plastic tape up against the square shoulder of the stem and pin it down to the dowel. Wind it round and along so it forms a tight spiral along the length of the dowel, and then, holding the tape in one hand to maintain tension, unwind it and mark out the thread as it unravels.

To cut the thread you will need a V-shaped carving tool, which is used by resting it on the toolrest and feeding it along the dowel at the same time as

you rotate the candlestick stem with your other hand.

Cut the thread between the lines with a single V-cut of the chisel or form it using several passes if the wood proves particularly stubborn.

Sanding and polishing

Wear a face mask when sanding, so you don't inhale the fine dust. Begin with a fairly coarse abrasive, about 150 grit, to smooth out any unevenness and remove any dimples and rings left by the gouge. I use a flexible cloth-backed aluminium oxide abrasive which is ideal for working in and out of the concave curves and hollows.

Take care not to over-sand, as you don't want to loose any of the fullness of the shapes or crispness of the edges. When you are satisfied all tool marks are gone, change to smoother grades.

With fine-grained wood like mopane, you will probably need to finish off with at least a 600-grit abrasive, perhaps even a 1000 grade, to remove the last trace of the coarser abrasives.

With a decorative turning project, there's no need to use the modern durable plastic finishes used to protect the work from coffee or water stains.

I like old-fashioned shellac French polish, which can be wiped into the tight crevices in the mouldings and, after a few minutes' drying, can be wax-polished, preferably with a hard pure carnauba friction wax.

This is applied with the lathe running, by pressing the wax against the revolving work. When enough has been rubbed over the surface, it's burnished to a high gloss using soft flannelette cotton cloth. ■

Cutting the screw threads with a V-shape carving tool.

Crunch time

Salt and pepper mills can be bought in most department stores and kitchen shops, but it's much nicer – and more of a challenge – to make your own

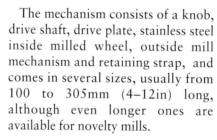

Salt and pepper mills.

Before the invention of the pepper mill, ground pepper was produced by placing the corns inside a perforated metal ball, or quern, containing a marble, and pulverizing them through shaking. Imagine the clatter at our forebears' dinner tables. It probably threw more pepper into the air than onto the food.

Fortunately, today's mechanisms make getting pepper onto the plate less noisy and problematic. Salt and pepper mills are standard in most kitchens and on dining tables. You can, of course, buy them in most department stores and specialist kitchen shops, but they're nice to make.

The mechanism consists of a knob, drive shaft, drive plate, stainless steel inside milled wheel, outside mill mechanism and retaining strap, and comes in several sizes, usually from 100 to 305mm (4–12in) long, although even longer ones are available for novelty mills.

Wood

Beech is traditionally used for making mills, but almost any dense tough-grained wood will do, so long as it's solid enough to provide a firm bed

for the two small screws which secure the outside mill wheel. The mills shown here have been made from afzelia, a tough, rather fibrous hardwood from Africa, which sands easily and can yield a very bright finish if needed.

It has a fairly pungent, peppery smell when fresh cut, which may need a little time to lose, before it can be used for food. The finished mill will need a wide base so that it's stable when standing upright. I have used two blocks, 70mm square by 240mm long (2¾ x 9½in), to make the 200mm (8in) mills. The salt mill is the same size as the pepper mill and the following techniques apply to both.

Mill body

Saw off about 50mm (2in) from the end of each block to make the mill heads and put them to one side. Place the block of wood for the body of the pepper mill onto the lathe between centres and set the speed at 2000rpm.

Using a roughing gouge, reduce the work to a cylinder along its length, apart from a short section at one end which you leave with its square

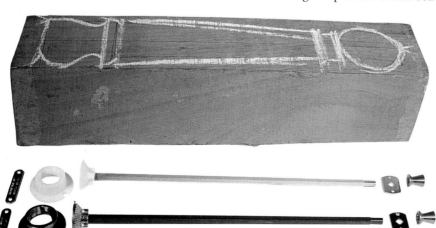

Block of afzelia with the salt and pepper mill mechanisms laid out.

corners intact. These corners will create a wider area of contact with the face of the chuck jaws, increasing the gripping power of the chuck, important when holding long pieces of work.

With a freshly ground and honed beading and parting tool, make a straightforward parting cut through the revolving corners of the workpiece and form a correctly-sized spigot to fit your chuck jaws. Turn the tool on its side and scrape the dovetail recess into the spigot's shoulder. This will give a positive purchase for the chuck jaws when they are closed.

Essential tool

The beading and parting tool is one of my most essential tools, and comes in two standard sizes – the 10mm (⅜in) and the 6mm (¼in). It is basically a square-sectioned chisel, ground from both sides to create a chisel-shaped tip.

When sharpening this tool, the edge must be accurately ground straight across, so the corners are sharp and square. A few strops across the oil-stone will make it razor sharp. With the tool kept in this condition, it can do a variety of tasks.

Grinding jig

Grinding tools without burning or mis-shaping the edges or points is difficult, and most woodturners use some form of jig to help them. My grinding jig has been modified several times over the years, but the latest version is the most convenient to use. To make it you will need a small sheet of ply or chipboard to form a solid table for laying the tool handle onto.

Cut out a section so it projects around the sides of the grinding wheel and, with blocks beneath, fix it firmly at a sloping angle of about 80° to the wheel face. You don't have to be exact about the angle or size of the table, so long as it supports the tool at a comfortable working position. Glue a horizontal strip about 50mm (2in) from the edge of the grindstone, which will keep the toolrest blocks in position. The success of the jig relies largely on the shape of the toolrest blocks, which have a central ridge and

Cutting the spigot on the end of the blank.

a section cut away so that the tool blade can be supported close to the grind wheel.

This shape, more importantly, provides a projecting platform which prevents the rest from toppling into the grind wheel under the pressure of the tool. Make several toolrest blocks of varying heights, and when a block is found to produce a suitable bevel angle for a tool, carefully label it so it can be easily found when it is needed again.

Mill body continued

With the wooden block held securely in the chuck, and the tailstock brought up as extra support, slice the end with a 6mm (¼in) bowl gouge, so it has a clean, smooth finish and is slightly concave.

Cut most of the recess for the flange of the outside part of the grinding mechanism with a 38mm (1½in) saw-toothed centre drill. The drill is held in the tailstock which is wound in, with the lathe running at its lowest speed.

Widen and deepen the recess with a square scraper, so the full width of the flange and also the retaining strap can be adequately accommodated clear of the base of the mill. When this has been done, bring the tailstock, with a revolving centre fitted, back into use so it supports the end of the work again.

You can now start shaping the outside of the pepper mill's body. The design is up to you, but you will need to disguise the join between the head and base with a moulding or some other detail, if it's to look good.

Cutting the dovetail on the spigot using the beading tool on its side.

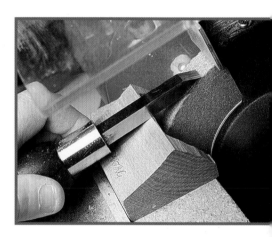
Grinding the bevel on a beading and parting tool using a grinding jig.

Slicing the end of the body smooth with tailstock still used as support.

A pepper mill made in an irregular flowing shape, lacking clear reference points from which to take readings, causes problems when it comes to duplicating it for the salt mill. I've avoided a very ornamental shape for my mill, staying with traditional mouldings with recognisable, easily reproduced forms.

For making copies, as well as using vernier callipers, which are used for testing spindle and recess diameters, I find odd-leg callipers ideal for accurately transferring the work's lateral dimensions .

The pear or vase shape of the lower half of the mill body is formed above a 15mm (⅝in) high half-bead at the base of the mill, by first slicing two V-cuts, one at the base and another at the top of the vase. These cuts are made by holding a skew chisel with the longest side underneath and feeding it into the wood, first on one side of a mark, then the other, removing a triangular section of waste.

This is repeated until you get the desired width and depth of the V-cut. The round shape of the pear, that intersects with the point of the lower V-cut, is made with the beading and parting tool using the same technique as when forming a bead. To form the curved shape of the bead, a beading and parting tool is again used.

This is placed nearly flat onto the work surface with only the corner of the tool engaged, so that it lifts the fibres of wood slightly. The tool is then rolled round in a series of fine cuts, starting at the bead's crown and ending where the bead intersects the point of

Drilling the recess for the flange of the mill mechanism.

the V-cut. Cut first one side and then the other until a perfect round is formed. This technique is used for making the half-bead at the base of the mill. The neck of the vase is hollowed out with a spindle gouge, used on its side to start the cut and then twisted round as the cut proceeds, so that it pans out at the bottom of the hollow. This is repeated on each side until the depth of the hollow is reached. The same tool is then used to join the sweeping curve of the hollow with the convex curve formed by the beading and parting tool.

At the top of the pepper mill, make a parting cut to define the mill's body

Widening the recess for the flange of the mill mechanism with a scraper.

length, using a standard 3mm (⅛in) parting tool. Then reduce the area at the top of the body to a series of square-stepped sections, using the beading and parting tool. Create a square fillet at the top of the mill, with a narrower square neck section below, then a wider square section for a half-bead. Below this, reduce the top of the main taper to the neck's diameter.

This is all done by parting down with a beading and parting tool, which is then used to form the curve of the half-bead. The long, straight taper is cut using a freshly sharpened roughing gouge to remove the bulk of the waste.

If rippling occurs along the length of

Rounding off the base of the pear shape with the beading tool.

Forming the hollow neck of the pear shape with a spindle gouge.

Cutting the top of the mill body into square sections.

Turning the square section into a half-bead shape.

ABOVE **Forming the tapered waist of the mill with the roughing gouge.**

RIGHT **Lateral cuts with a beading and parting tool to improve the finish.**

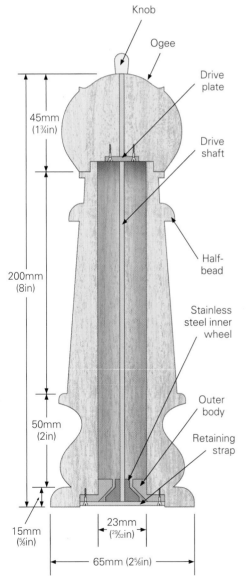

Knob

Ogee

Drive plate

Drive shaft

45mm
(1¾in)

200mm
(8in)

Half-bead

Stainless steel inner wheel

Outer body

50mm
(2in)

Retaining strap

15mm
(⅝in)

23mm
(²⁹⁄₃₂in)

65mm (2⅝in)

the taper, you can easily remove it with a sanding block, or by using the beading and parting tool to flatten off. This is done by feeding the tool laterally along the length of the taper with the only the corner engaged.

To sand the work you must wear an effective dust mask. I use J-flex aluminum oxide cloth abrasive to sand, which is good on afzelia. I start with 100 grit and work my way through 240, ending with 400 grit, using each successive grade to remove the scratch marks of the previous one.

When sanding, look for the stream of dust, the best sign that the abrasive is working properly. When the steam disappears, change your abrasive to avoid overheating the work surface.

One of the best and most durable waterproof finishes is two coats of acrylic sealer, applied with a brush or cloth and rubbed down with Webrax (an abrasive product like a nylon pan scrub). After the two sealing coats have dried, apply a lighter finishing coat with a clean cloth.

Hollowing the body

After sanding and polishing, mount a 22mm (⅞in) drill in the headstock and drill a hole through the mill's body, stopping just before the drill point reaches the face of the chuck. Unless you have an extra-long auger for doing this job, you will need to fit your drill with an extension rod.

Fixing the extension drill into a Jacobs chuck.

When making this hole with the saw-toothed centre, the hole must be cleared every 25mm (1in) or so by stopping the lathe and withdrawing and cleaning the drill.

You may be irritated to find the hole is not quite big enough to take the

Slicing the base face of the pepper mill head smooth.

Testing that the base of the mill fits into the head.

Cutting the recess for the drive plate of the mill mechanism.

mechanism and that more work with the scraper or abrasive is needed.

It's better to do this than use the next drill size up, because a 1in drill may reduce the shelf's strength so much that the screws which must lock the body of the mechanism may work free when the mill is being used.

Determining the size of the head.

Drilling the hole for the drive shaft.

Once the hole is complete, all that remains is to use the beading and parting tool to part down and form a spigot at the top of the mill's body which will locate the head on the body. Then part off the body with the standard parting tool.

Making the head

Prepare the block of wood for the head in the same way as for the body, and fit it in the chuck. Slice the face smooth with the 6mm (¼in) bowl gouge. Using a square scraper, scrape a shallow square recess for the spigot of the mill body, and check it rotates well.

Make another recess, this time for the circular drive plate, which must be centred in the floor of the head. Carefully calculate the length of the head by placing the base with the grinding mechanism and shaft up alongside and marking it off.

Part down, leaving a spindle thick enough to hold the work while it is shaped. You can do a lot of the broad shaping of the head while it is held in this way, using the bowl gouge, but the top of the head has to be done with the work held in a jam chuck.

After parting off completely, form a mandrel on the waste wood left in the chuck, so that a push fit is formed for the head. With the head held securely on the mandrel, drill a 6mm (¼in) centre hole for the drive shaft through the centre of the head. Angle the toolrest so it better supports the tools while working on the top of the head, and form a ball shape, using the corner of the beading and parting tool.

Shaping the top of the head.

Roll the handle of the tool, with the edge on its side, removing one thin slice at a time, as if you were making a large bead. I've made a small fillet or step with the corner of the beading and parting tool held at a cutting angle, with the edge square to the work.

The spigot formed on the top of the head is then re-shaped into a shallow ogee shape, using the point of a spindle gouge held on its side. And your salt and pepper mills are complete! ■

Light-weight lamp

Shorter than the usual standard lamp, this design is ideal for use as a bedside or reading light

The piece of English oak from which I turned the base for this standard lamp looked unpromising at first. But we woodturners are a resourceful lot, and I was able to put it to good use by placing the faults underneath, where they wouldn't show, or on the top outside edge, where they were removed with the waste.

When using such timber you must be sure, of course, that the structure of the wood is not so badly affected by splits that it's in danger of disintegrating on the lathe. Select a slow 500rpm lathe speed, wear a face shield, and frequently check the solidity of the workpiece as you cut.

Traditional standard lamps were tall and made for standing in the corner of the room to add to the general lighting. But the recent fashion for more localised interior light has boosted interest in shorter lamps. This lamp is about 1m high (approximately 40in), producing a low-level light ideal for use beside the bed or for armchair reading.

To make it you will need a disc 330mm diameter by 65mm (13 x 2⅝in) thick for the base and two lengths 500mm long by 65mm by 65mm (19⅝ x 2⅝ x 2⅝in) for the

Photo 1 **Screwing the faceplate to the back of the work**.

column, plus a short piece of 70mm (2¾in) stock for the feet.

Bottom of base

To flatten the bottom of the base, secure a faceplate in the centre of the disc with at least four screws. I put waste wood between faceplate and workpiece to spread the screws apart, so the holes will lie in the area where the waste is removed (photo 1).

The screws need to bed into the disc to a depth of about 15mm (⅝in) to hold the work safely, though there are no hard and fast rules about this – just make sure it's good and solid.

Set the lathe's headstock and toolrest attachment in the bowl-turning mode, to provide adequate clearance for wide-diameter work. Mount the disc onto the headstock,

set the toolrest along the workface about 13mm (½in) below centre, check the toolrest levers are tight and that nothing obstructs the swing of the work, stand to one side and switch on.

Use a freshly sharpened 13mm (½in) superflute bowl gouge to cut the bottom of the base smooth and flat (photo 2). Use the gouge slightly on its side and feed it slowly across the face, taking light cuts until the old surface has been removed.

If the disc is very uneven you will need to keep the gouge steady by holding the shaft securely against the toolrest, with the handle butt supported against the front of your leg. With this grip you should be able to prevent the tool moving in and out with the uneven surface of the work.

Photo 2 **Flattening the bottom of the lamp base**.

Photo 3 **Testing the flatness.**

Photo 4 **Marking out for the faceplate position**.

Photo 5 **Cutting the concave shape in the top half of the base.**

Photo 6 **Lateral cut with the corner of a beading and parting tool to form a shallow bead shape.**

Photo 7 **Cleaning the corner with a dovetail scraper.**

At this time screws can become dislodged, so listen out for any low-pitched rattle or rumble, the tell-tale sounds of the disc working loose. Test the bottom of the base for flatness (photo 3) and mark a line around the edge of the base to position the feet of the lamp stand, plus a series of rings for re-positioning the faceplate in the centre (photo 4).

Shaping the base

After using the pencil rings to centre the faceplate, screw it directly to the disc, mount the work on the lathe and flatten the face, following the same procedure as before.

Leave a 65mm (2⅝in) flat area in the centre of the disc, and roughly taper the rest of the base towards the edge, with the bowl gouge.

Form the concave shape at the top of the tapered base using the same gouge, which will cut cleanly when it is used in the direction away from the centre – with the grain (photo 5). The tool angle is pitched back so that the

bevel lies flat against the work surface and acts like the sole of a plane.

At the foot of this gentle curve, cut a step or fillet with a beading and parting tool, making a parting cut by holding the tool at 45° to the work with the cutting edge horizontal.

Cut the shallow convex shape which will form the top half of the ogee, using the same technique. You can improve the quality of the surface by using the corner of the tool to cut laterally (photo 6), but don't try to roll the chisel on its side, because this will almost certainly cause the edge to dig.

This occurs partly because the tool wanders off course in the middle of its cut, due to the length of time it takes for the workpiece to complete its revolution and also, probably

more importantly, due to the grain fibres not lying in a formation that allows them to be cut off cleanly. (See 'Grain direction' panel on page 59).

I used the point of my dovetail scraper to clean up the inside corner where the top of the ogee meets the fillet (photo 7). To form the bottom half of the ogee, use a small 6mm (¼in) bowl gouge or spindle gouge (photo 8).

Cut another step or fillet, and form a quadrant on the outer edge of the base, with the same small bowl gouge (photo 9). Shape most of the piece with the toolrest positioned along the work face. Don't cut all the way round or you'll fray the unsupported fibres of the rim.

Position the toolrest right round at an angle from the back, so you can

LEFT Photo 8 **Cutting the hollow of the lower half of the ogee using a small bowl gouge.**

Photo 9 **Forming the quadrant on the edge of the lamp base.**

Photo 10 **Cutting from the other side to complete the quadrant.**

Photo 11 **Widening the hole in the base with the square scraper.**

finish the shape cleanly from the opposite direction (photo 10).

Make the 40mm (1⅝in) wide by 50mm (2in) deep hole for the column using a 13mm (½in) round scraper to remove most of the waste, and widen and straighten the sides with a square scraper (photo 11).

If you are using a standard scraper, supplied with a rectangle cross section, you will need to grind away one of the sides to produce a relieved edge so that the bottom corner cannot bind on the side of the hole.

Remove the work from the lathe, but leave the lamp base on its

faceplate in case the size of the hole for the column needs enlarging.

The column

The standard lamp column is made in two equal sections with a small bead and fillet moulding to hide the joint. Find the centres of each section and mount them, in turn, on the lathe. Turn them down to a cylinder with a large roughing gouge.

Don't be too fussy about reducing the work completely to a cylinder at this stage, as the column will be re-centred after the drilling stage and will probably need re-trueing.

To make the hole for the flex, mount a section between centres using a hollow cone centre in the tailstock. Run the lathe at about 800rpm and feed your lamp auger through the hole in the tailstock about 20 or 30mm (¾–1⅛in) at a time, withdrawing the point each time to clean the flute.

You can see in photo 12 that the hollow centre I use has been modified with a large hole drilled through the side, which allows the waste to clear without clogging the tailstock barrel.

This is very important, because any delay that occurs while boring can cause the hollow centre to overheat, burning the work and reducing tailstock pressure so that the work loosens. I have also installed a

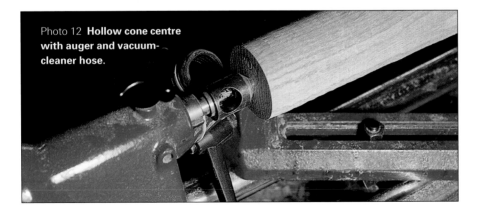

Photo 12 **Hollow cone centre with auger and vacuum-cleaner hose.**

Photo 13 **Fitting the counter-bore.**

Photo 14 **Cutting the dowel.**

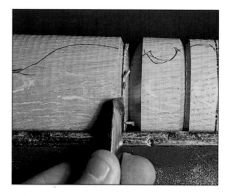

Photo 15 **Making a V-cut with skew chisel.**

Photo 16 **Forming the bulbous vase section with a beading and parting tool.**

Photo 17 **Cutting hollow neck of vase with a 6mm (¼in) bowl gouge.**

vacuum-cleaner hose, close to the hollow centre, so waste is drawn away as it leaves the hole.

Once you've bored half-way, turn the section round, remove the drive centre and replace with a counter-bore (photo 13). The counter-bore has four drive prongs and a central pilot which slides into the hole and centres the workpiece.

Bore the other half of the column in the same way, and if all goes well your holes will meet in the middle.

I usually take the column section off the lathe at this stage and check that the electric flex will pass through. After repeating the process for the other section, you should have a hole running down the centre of each so that when they are joined together they form a continuous cavity up which the flex can run.

Lower column mouldings

To make the mouldings on the lower column section, use the counter-bore in the drive end and replace the standard revolving centre in the tailstock to support the work.

Trim it back to a balanced cylinder with the roughing gouge, and mark the column shape. A rough sketch before turning helps me get the proportions of the mouldings right.

Use the beading and parting tool to cut the dowel at the base of the column to the same size as the hole in the lamp base (photo 14).

The pear, or vase, shape is formed by first making the deep V-cut at the top of the shape (photo 15) and a smaller one at the base, using the skew chisel.

V-cuts are made by feeding the lower point of the skew chisel into the side of the work, first on one side of the V and then the other, removing the triangle section of waste. A series of cuts are made in this way, until you get the V-cut size you want.

Cut the bulbous shape of the 'vase' with the beading and parting tool (photo 16), using the same lateral cutting technique used on the shallow bead of the base, but twist the tool on its side to make a much more rounded bead and a cleaner cut.

Form the beads above and below the vase section using the same method, and hollow out the neck of the vase with the small bowl gouge. This tool is used on its side to start the cut and twisted round during the cut, so that it pans out at the bottom

of the hollow (photo 17).

Repeat this on each side until the depth of the hollow is reached. Form the concave moulding that lies directly above the vase with the same gouge and technique.

Reduce the diameter of the top of the column with the roughing gouge to about 47mm (1⅞in), and cut another dowel the same diameter as the counter-bore. Make a small concave radius with the gouge, leaving a small fillet on the end of the column. Form the long, tapered middle section of the column using a sharpened roughing gouge.

Counter-bore

The counter-bore is used to drill a hole in the bottom end of the top column to form a joint with the lower section dowel. With the lathe set at the slowest speed, no more than 500rpm, position the counter-bore's pilot into the auger hole and hold the section in your gloved hand while winding in the tailstock.

When the hole is deep enough, switch off the lathe, let go of the

Photo 18 **Making the bead on the base of the top column.**

Photo 19 **Reducing the top to square sections.**

Photo 20 **An alternative method of forming a bead.**

work, tighten the tailstock and the counter-bore reverts to a drive centre again.

Reduce the diameter at the base of the column and, after squaring off the end, form a 55mm (2¼in) diameter bead (photo 18). To enable the bead to sit neatly on the fillet of the lower column and hide the joint, you may need to undercut the end surface.

Slice the top of the column clean and true, using a skew chisel, taking care to avoid scoring the side of the revolving centre or damaging the point of the skew. Cut with the longest edge of the chisel held downwards and take three or four thin slices to remove all signs of the drive centre.

Top column mouldings

The mouldings at the top of the column are produced by reducing the entire area to a series of steps and square sections, starting with the beading and parting tool (photo 19). These are then left in the form of fillets or, by rounding them, beads.

An alternative method of bead forming is shown in photo 20, in which the beading and parting tool is used with its cutting edge horizontal so the tool approaches the work at various angles and creates a series of facets. These are later rounded off with abrasive. This technique may lack sophistication, but it gets results. The same thing could be said for my preference for using the roughing gouge over the skew when

Photo 21 **Forming the radius on the foot.**

forming the tapers. The gouge may not produce the immaculate finish achievable with the skew, but it's much more stable and, if freshly sharpened, gives a finish which, if not perfect, can be quickly remedied with abrasive.

The five bun feet, 70mm (2¾in) diameter by about 30mm (1⅛in) thick, are turned from one length of oak. After parting down between each foot section, use a spindle gouge to form a small radius in the top half of each foot (photo 21). The feet are attached around the underside of the base and provide clearance for the electric flex.

Sand the lamp stand with 150-grit, then 240 and 400 abrasive, before wax-polishing by applying a generous layer of Briwax with the lathe at rest. Buff with a soft clean cloth.

Before assembling and gluing together, feed the electric flex through and fit the bulb holder in the top (photo 22). ■

Photo 22 **Testing the fit.**

Grain direction

Grain direction radically influences the way we use tools to cut, slice and form shapes on the lathe.

In spindle turning, where the grain runs along the work's central axis, chisels are used tilted on their sides to make penetrating cuts, and flat on the apex of the work for planing cuts. These techniques create the kind of crisp spindle work which is the hall-mark of the proficient woodturner. But these same techniques, if applied to work where the grain runs diametrically across the axis of the workpiece, as is the case with this standard lamp, would not only be ineffectual, but dangerous.

F lower vases are made in most materials – glass, pottery, plastic and earthenware – but rarely turned in wood. I lined this one with a glass jar to hold the water, but modern waterproof finishes may make it possible to have a durable vase without a container inside.

This 150mm diameter by 200mm tall (6 x 8in) vase is made from a semi-seasoned cherry-tree log, and is close to the limit of what can be

How to turn a vase lined with a glass jar to hold flowers

Blooming beautiful

hollowed on an average-sized lathe using standard turning tools.

It was hollowed from both ends, using 13mm (½in) round and 25mm (1in) square scrapers, which had both been fitted with extra-long handles to provide more leverage.

Photo 1 **Using the Perspex centring device to centre each end of the log.**

The other tools used consisted of 38 and 19mm (1½ and ¾in) roughing gouges, 6mm (¼in) and 10mm (⅜in) bowl gouges, 10mm (⅜in) beading and parting tool, 13mm (½in) oval skew chisel, and 3mm (⅛in) parting tool.

Setting up

To quickly find the centres of each end of the log, you may like to make a handy centring device like the one shown (photo 1). It's made from a scrap of Perspex with a series of scored circles radiating from a centre hole. You simply place it so that you

can see through, find the nearest circle that corresponds to the outer edge of the log, and make a mark through the hole drilled in the centre of the device.

Use a soft-headed hammer to punch the four-prong drive centre into one end of the log (photo 2). This supports and drives the work while it's held in place by the revolving centre in the tailstock end.

I always use a revolving tail centre for between-centre work because, unlike a dead centre, it spins round with the work and doesn't burn the wood. To test that the workpiece is

Photo 2 **Driving in the four-prong centre with a soft-headed hammer.**

Photo 3 **Testing that the workpiece is tight on the lathe.**

Photo 4 **Turning the work to a cylinder.**

ABOVE Photo 5 **Flatten off one end with the beading and parting tool.**

RIGHT Photo 6 **Fixing on the faceplate.**

Photo 7 **Slicing the end of the work square with the 6mm (¼in) bowl gouge.**

Photo 8 **Forming the overall shape of the vase.**

tight enough, lock the headstock with a spanner or tommy bar and try twisting the work by hand (photo 3). If the work turns round or becomes dislodged from its centres, then it will need a few more turns of the tailstock hand wheel.

Position the height of the toolrest so that the edge of the gouge, when used at a 45° cutting angle, contacts the side of the work at centre height. Set the lathe speed to about 500rpm and stand clear before switching on, then if all goes well, reposition yourself so you are facing the lathe and able to move freely from side to side, without losing your balance (photo 4).

I turned the log to a true cylinder with the large 38mm (1½in) roughing gouge, ideal for cutting this regular-shaped log with its soft, even grain. If there had been any hard knots or troublesome grain to deal with, I would have chosen the 13mm (½in) long and strong bowl gouge, with its smaller, more controllable cut.

With the handle held against your body, rest the blade of the roughing-down gouge on the toolrest and slowly bring the edge of the tool into the path of the work. Hold the tool firmly down onto the toolrest and, with a series of shallow cuts, gradually reduce the log to a smooth cylinder.

As you work, periodically move the toolrest in, to maintain an adequate leverage over the tool. Use your knuckles against the back edge of the toolrest to control the depth of cut.

Next, part down with the beading and parting tool at one end of the log to form a flat surface (photo 5). Leave a small spigot so that the workpiece can be centred when it is screwed onto a faceplate (photo 6). The screws need to penetrate the end grain at least 13mm (½in) to be sure of a firm grip. Don't worry about wasting wood, because the screw holes will

come out when the vase is hollowed. You can, of course, use a chucking method, but a faceplate will hold the workpiece closer to the headstock, giving more rigidity.

Flattening the base

With the section firmly held on the lathe, set the toolrest at 45° to the end of the work and slice the bottom of the vase smooth with a 6mm (¼in) bowl gouge (photo 7). To make this facing-off cut, the tool is angled to one side so that the bevel lies parallel to the end of the workpiece.

The gouge is fed forward with the handle of the tool held against the body with the right hand, while the shaft is passed through the guiding fingers of the left hand. With a freshly sharpened gouge there should be little resistance. Apply only as much pressure as is needed to keep the edge

Photo 9 **Forming the ovolo moulding on the plinth with the 3mm (⅛in) parting tool.**

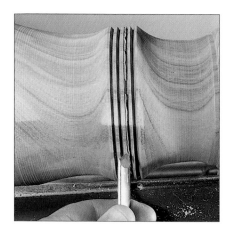

Photo 10 **Making the row of V-cuts to form the reeds.**

Photo 11 **Shaping the set of reeds with the parting tool.**

Photo 12 & 13 **Drilling out the bottom of the base.**

of the tool in place.

Once the tool is cutting smoothly, it's really a matter of feel, although a lot can be read from the shavings, which should flow in a continuous string, especially if the timber used is a little green, like this cherry.

Starting the cut off is often a problem for beginners, as there is no support for the bevel at this point and the tool is prone to slip back and dig into the corner of the work. To avoid this, position the tool to take a depth of cut of no more that a millimetre or so, and bring the cutting edge into play very slowly while anchoring the shaft firmly onto the toolrest.

The vase shape, with its simple concave curves, is formed using the 19mm (¾in) roughing gouge (photo 8). Remember that to avoid spiral patterns occurring when you are forming shapes on a large diameter, your lateral cutting movements will need to be slowed down to allow

enough time for a complete revolution of the workpiece.

Plinth and ovolo moulding

Form the square plinth at the base of the vase with the beading and parting tool by cutting a small square step about 25mm (1in) from the base. Then use the standard 3mm (⅛in) parting tool to form the ovolo (photo 9) This tool is narrow enough to start the radius of the shape in the shoulder of the step. Roll the tool in a series of cuts and gradually the round shape of the moulding will form. The important thing is to take very fine cuts and only use the extreme corner of the tool.

Reeds

Mark out the central band of the vase for a row of narrow reeds, and then use the skew chisel to make shallow V-cuts on each line. Use the lower point of the tool and make a cut at an angle, first on one side of the

line and then on the other, removing a thin slice each time (photo 10). Take off the corners of the reeds with the parting tool (photo 11), but leave the final shaping until the sanding stage.

Hollowing

To hollow one end of the vase, create a pilot hole using a saw-toothed centre drill held in the tailstock (photos 12 and 13).

Remove the bulk of the waste using a square scraper in a forward motion, sliding the tool down the side of the hole like a reamer (photo 14). By feeding the tool along the side of the hole made by the drill, and only removing a small amount of wood at a time, the hole is slowly opened to the required width.

The full width of the scraper's cutting edge must be prevented from biting into the end face of the hole at all costs, as this will cause a tremendous snatch and may dislodge the workpiece. For hollowing 100mm (4in) away from the support of the

Photo 14 **Widening out the hole with the scraper**.

Photo 15 **Cutting the groove for the floor of the vase**.

toolrest, a long tool handle is essential to exert the necessary leverage. Make sure the inside walls of the vase at the base are parallel.

Position the toolrest inside the opening and make a 3mm (⅛in) deep housing groove about 3mm from the vase's base, using the parting tool (photo 15). Remove the work from the lathe and faceplate, and fit it onto the lathe using a mandrel made from waste wood (photo 16). A tight fit on the mandrel makes it possible to hollow the mouth of the vase with the work held by friction alone. But to be more secure, run a line of hot glue between the edge of the mandrel and the top of the pot where they meet (photo 17). This will hold the work much more securely while you hollow the mouth of the vase.

Drill out as before (photo 18) and, if you are using a glass liner, form an opening wide enough to take the jar, allowing plenty of slack for wall shrinkage. Make the inside shape follow the line of the outside (photo

Using green wood

Well-seasoned timber in large dimensions is not cheap, so learning how to process the wood yourself, from the branches and trunks of small trees such as apple and pear, is one way of keeping costs down.

Orchards and copses are periodically thinned out by farmers, and timber from these is often obtained for the asking. And when it becomes known that you are a woodturner, you will have neighbours and friends coming round with odd cuttings from their garden trees which can be ideal for smaller projects.

Another potential source is your local supplier of firewood for woodburning stoves. Such firms usually have a large stockpile of mixed hardwoods and – especially if you order a load of logs for the fire at the same time -- will probably be happy to let you root around for a suitable piece.

Finding space for your freshly cut logs can be a problem, but try and keep them in long lengths. The main thing is to store them out of the rain and away from the sun for six months or so. This will minimise decay, and allow the timber to dry out slowly.

Sealing the ends of the logs with paint, wax or end seal safeguards the wood from too much end-grain splitting. You can leave them as they are, unprotected, which will usually only lose you about 100mm (4in) at each end while the timber between should be usable.

Think carefully about what you want to make with your green timber. Although thin branches up

Using green logs is cheaper.

to 60mm (2⅜in) can be used for chair legs and similar spindle work without too much risk of splitting, larger-diameter timber will invariably crack down its side – usually within days of its being turned.

One way of overcoming this problem with semi-seasoned timber is to hollow the workpiece's central core, giving space for the wood at the circumference to shrink into.

The final drying process occurs after the work has been finished. A layer of polish will also help to protect it. As an extra precaution, you can make separate tops and floors for your hollow table lamps, boxes or vases, out of seasoned wood which are then fitted into housing grooves before the work has shrunk.

When converting round butts into square stock and small bowl blanks, a chainsaw and large bandsaw are very useful, but need expert advice before they can be handled safely.

But simple hand tools can also be used. A bowsaw, if kept sharp, will make short work of cutting through small logs, and keep you fit too.

You can use wooden wedges to split logs, a practice which goes back to the last ice age. But this may be taking tradition too far.

19), testing the thickness of the walls from time to time between your fingers as you work.

Sanding & polishing

When you happy with your vase shape, you can sand it smooth. When sanding, I use an aluminium oxide

that is resin-bonded onto a flexible cloth backing. I start with 80 grit and follow up with 240, which removes the scratches of the coarser abrasive.

If you have any problems with the wood being too wet, a hair dryer will dry the surface, although I find

Photo 16 **Jam-fitting the work on the mandrel**.

Photo 17 **Applying a glue joint to hold the work more securely**.

Photo 18 **Drilling out the top of the vase**.

that the friction caused by sanding is usually quite sufficient by itself. I then give the work a light rub with 350 or 400 grit to be sure of obtaining a fault-free finish when the polish is applied.

Because of the wood's probable contact with water, I use a cellulose sealer to finish the vase. This is best applied quickly with a paintbrush, using a sheet of hardboard to protect the lathe bed from any splashes and drops. Then, before it dries, the whole surface of the work can be wiped off with a clean cotton cloth, which will absorb any surplus polish and leave a completely even coat.

This method avoids the overlapping which can occur when the polish is applied with a cloth or

rubber only, and can be repeated to create any thickness of finish required.

To make a watertight container in wood, you will need to wait until the vase has settled to its final shape before coating the inside with a waterproof finish. There are a number of finishes which are extremely water-resistant. Rustin's plastic coating and acrylic sealer are two which spring to mind.

Apply two or three coats with a brush, working the sealer into the edge of the floor where it meets the walls. Leave it to dry thoroughly before adding water.

Floor board

Any piece of 6mm (¼in) ply will do for the floor, but I prefer to make

mine out of thicknessed oak board left over from a cabinetmaking project. Stick the disc onto a faceplate using double-sided carpet tape, and trim and chamfer to the final size with a gouge (photo 20), so that it produces a tight fit through the hole in the base of the vase. When the floor piece is the right size, prise it off the faceplate, squeeze it through the base opening and manoeuvre it into the groove (photo 21).

At first the floor board will only become loosely trapped, but before many days have passed, all slop or play will be eliminated as the sides of the pot shrink around it. It may be necessary to ease it in from time to time as the pot assumes its final dimensions. ■

Photo 19 **Scraping the inside wall of the vase to thickness**.

Photo 20 **Cutting the disc down to size to make a floor board for the vase**.

Photo 21 **Fitting the floor board into the groove in the base**.

Weather eyes

This weather set houses a trio of instruments which could make BBC weatherman Michael Fish completely redundant

The completed weather instrument set.

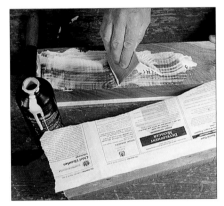

Photo 1 **Gluing up.**

Photo 2 **Determining the centre of the work.**

This weather set consists of a barometer, hygrometer and thermometer – a trio of hemispheres positioned along a central stem. I used figured English walnut for the frame, a timber which, when taken from an area in the base of the tree, can be spectacularly rich in colour and the equal of any 'exotic' hardwood.

Although more difficult to work than plain, straight-grained timber, it rewards well the time and trouble taken, and the finished work looks good in almost any surroundings.

Split turning

A method called 'split turning' has been used to produce the flat faces and back of the frame. It's possible with this technique to make two weather sets back to back, but I've chosen to make just one, and have used waste wood to balance the work and stop the edges breaking or being worn away during sanding.

You will need a piece of walnut 370mm long x 100mm wide x 50mm thick (14⅝ x 4 x 2in) to make this

combination frame. The backing board is made from a piece of 50mm (2in) thick pine and the front strip is about 20mm (¾in) thick.

Make sure surfaces to be glued are perfectly flat before applying a coat of white PVA glue to each face (photo 1). Then slip a sheet of newspaper between, cramp the assembly together, and leave overnight for the glue to dry thoroughly.

Finding centres

Before mounting the work on the lathe, a little careful calculation is needed to ensure the area at the front of the frame is wide enough to take the full width of the mechanism.

Draw parallel lines corresponding to the outer edge of the barometer onto the end of the workpiece, so they pass through the joint between the front waste board and the walnut block used for the frame.

Then, using compasses, calculate the centres by drawing the largest circle the block will contain, so that the circumference intersects the lines where they cross the joint.

You can see that the centre of my assembly has come onto the walnut side of the joint (photo 2). When you are making only one weather set, this is an advantage in that the drive and tail centres which hold the work on the lathe don't act as wedges to drive the work and waste apart, which they would do if the centre fell on the joint between frame and backing block.

If you want to make two frames using the back-to-back spit-turning method, you will need to bridge across the join, with the four-prong drive centre at the headstock end of the work, and use a ring centre at the tailstock end.

After centre-punching one end with the drive centre, trim off any surplus waste wood so the assembly is well balanced, and mount it on the lathe between centres. Set the speed to about 1000rpm and adjust the toolrest so there is clearance for the corners of the block.

Wear a face shield

Wear a face shield at all times while shaping, sanding and polishing this project. There is always a danger in split turning that the glued-on waste piece can come apart if the glue joint is unsound.

Using a freshly sharpened roughing-down gouge, turn the work to a cylinder, by drawing the tool back and forth along the toolrest at a 45° cutting angle (photo 3).

Use external callipers to check the cylinder is the same diameter all the way along, and mark it out for the spheres (photo 4). The width of each sphere is calculated by the cylinder's

Photo 3 **Roughing off the corners.**

Photo 4 **Marking out the spheres.**

Photo 5 **Parting down on each side of the spheres.**

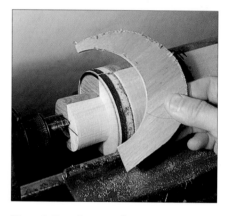

Photo 6 **Creating a perfect inside curve on the template.**

diameter, but the width and thickness of the spaces between is up to you.

Making the spheres

Cut down on each side of the spheres with the beading and parting tool (photo 5). Hold the tool firmly down onto the toolrest with the blade pointing up at a 45° cutting angle and slowly bring the edge into contact

with the wood. Feed the tool in at such a rate that it cuts smoothly and forms perfectly right-angled walls. The spindle left at the base of the cut creates the effect of a tapered central stem about 50mm (2in) in diameter running between the spheres of the weather frame.

Making a matching set of spheres is one of the most demanding

Photo 7 **First stage of making the sphere is cutting off the corners with a bowl gouge.**

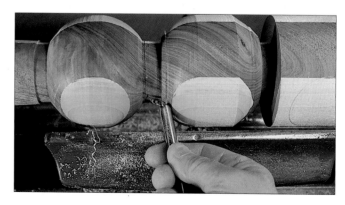

Photo 8 **The start of the curve cutting.**

Photo 9 **Trimming the last part of the curve with the spindle gouge.**

Photo 10 **Testing the sphere with the template.**

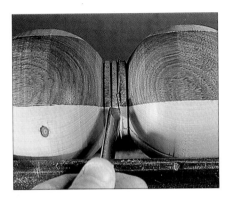

Photo 11 **Making the V-cuts for the reeds.**

Photo 12 **Finishing the reeds with the sanding wedge.**

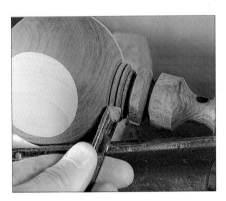

Photo 13 **Making a V-cut on the finial.**

operations in spindle turning – any deviation in size or shape will show up, especially when the spheres are close together.

To reduce some of the difficulties, make a template from a thin sheet of plywood or similar material by first marking out the curve of the sphere with a pair of compasses, and then cutting out the rough shape on the bandsaw (photo 6).

Sand the concave radius to its final shape, using a sanding drum temporarily fashioned from part of a slightly reduced cylindrical section of the workpiece, dressed with a narrow strip of abrasive. To fix the abrasive in place, apply and burnish double-sided tape to the back of it and to the drum before pressing the two surfaces firmly together.

Form the three spheres using a combination of the small 6mm (¼in) bowl gouge, ground straight across with the standard 45° bevel, and the 10mm (⅜in) spindle gouge, ground with a lady's-fingernail point.

Start with the bowl gouge and

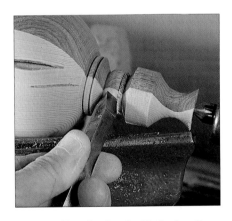

Photo 14 **Forming bead with the beading and parting tool.**

remove the corners of the section to form an octagon shape. Use the gouge slightly on its side, line up the bevel of the gouge with the direction you want to cut in, and slice off a thin section of material with each pass. Feed the gouge across the work with the bevel gently resting on the flat surface made by the previous cut (photo 7).

When it comes to forming the round sides of each hemisphere, use exactly the same gouge technique, but

Photo 15 **Forming the base of the onion shape of the finial.**

you must slowly bring the handle of the tool round in an arc as you make the cut, so the gouge's bevel always remains in line with the work surface.

Left-hand turning

Use a left-hand way of holding the gouge when you turn the left-hand hemisphere, which means holding the shaft of the gouge in your right hand and the handle in the left (photo 8).

Unless you are naturally left-handed

or ambidextrous, this will feel uncomfortable to begin with, but the advantage is that you can see the bevel of the tool and its angle to the work surface much more clearly. It also stops you exerting too much pressure at the top of the tool, pressing the bevel too hard against the work surface, which can lead to uneven cutting and spiral waves forming.

Use an open-handed grip if you can, so the tool can slide through your fingers, smoothly. A freshly sharpened gouge is essential for a clean finish, so don't be tempted into continuing your cut when the tool edge becomes dull.

You can twist the tool to change the edge presented to the work, so all the cutting edge of the gouge is used. Remember to keep the bevel flat against the work surface, whatever part of the edge you use.

Tight shoulder

Where each side of the sphere intersects the central shaft section is a tight shoulder where the blunt-nosed bowl gouge cannot go. A skew chisel could be used to slice into this, but the long-nosed spindle gouge is better, especially when there's a wavy grain to deal with (photo 9).

It's used, like the bowl gouge, with the bevel laid flat against the wall of the sphere, preventing the tool from diving into the wood's surface, the point of the gouge making the cut. A beading and parting tool will clean up any trace left in the internal corner.

As you come closer to realising the finished sphere, you will need to use whisker-thin cuts, alternating with stopping the lathe and checking the progress of the shape with the

Photo 16 **Parting in to form a section for the base moulding**.

Photo 17 **Forming the ogee shape of the base moulding**.

Photo 18 **Forming the point of the onion at the top of the finial**.

Photo 19 **Polishing the work with carnauba wax**.

template (photo 10). Don't get impatient and cut too much off at once - you can't put it back.

Stem decoration

I have decorated the central stem of my weather frame with bands of reeds. These are marked equidistantly, and V-cuts are formed on each line using a skew chisel (photo 11).

Use the lower point of the tool and make a cut at an angle, first on one side of the marked line and then on the other, removing a thin slice each time. The final shaping of the reeds

can be sanded using a thin wedge-shaped sanding block (photo 12).

Sanding

It's probably a good idea to get all the heavy sanding out of the way at this stage, before the thickness at both ends of the work is reduced to form the decorative finial and base pendant of the weather board.

Use 100-grade aluminium-oxide cloth-backed abrasive to sand out any unevenness from the spheres and also to shape the reeds. When sanding, use the template to support the back of

Photo 20 **Final parting off of the finished work**.

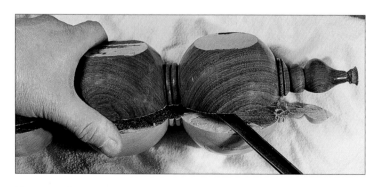

Photo 21 **Gently levering off the front and back plates of waste wood**.

Photos 22, 23 & 24 **Drilling out the housing hole for the mechanism, on the drill press, making sure that the work is firmly cramped first.**

the abrasive to preserve the shape.

Follow up with 250–300 grades of abrasive, and lastly smooth away any trace of the coarse abrasive with the 600-grit finishing grade. Be liberal with this, as when it is used blunt there is a danger of overheating the work surface, causing surface cracks – especially prevalent with fine-grained woods like walnut.

Finial & base pendant

When forming the decorative mouldings of the finial and base of the weather board, the skew chisel comes into its own, slicing the deep V-cuts needed before shaping can start (photo 13).

After forming two such cuts in the finial, use the beading and parting tool to make a bead (photo 14) and the lower half of the onion shape (photo 15). Bring the toolrest up close for support. Round the corners of the section between the V-cuts by twisting the tool so that the leading corner of the cutting edge engages with the wood and cuts by a series of controlled rolls of the tool.

Cut one side of the bead and then the other in the same way, in mirror form. Leave a substantial amount intact to support the workpiece while you carry out work at the other end of the frame.

First part down with the narrow parting tool to produce a square section to work on (photo 16), leaving an inch or so to drive and support the workpiece securely on the lathe. Use the spindle gouge on its side, and form an ogee shape by

arcing the tool handle back in one direction to form the concave hollow and then arcing in the opposite direction to form the convex dome of the ogee pendant (photo 17).

Do the last bit of turning to the top of the onion finial with the spindle gouge, reducing the point to 10mm (⅜in) thickness (photo 18).

Polishing

Final sanding and polishing should be done now, while the work is still supported on the lathe. Walnut responds well to most finishes, especially wax or natural oils such as tung oil or walnut oil. But the most aesthetically pleasing finish is shellac-based French polish.

Apply a coat or two with a clean cotton cloth and buff up with carnauba wax as soon as the shellac has dried. This hard wax is rubbed on with the lathe running, so that a thin coat is melted on the surface. This is burnished with soft flannelette-cotton cloth until it melts and spreads into the grain. It is then burnished with less pressure, to produce a spectacular shine (photo 19). Over time,

subsequent waxings with soft furniture wax will give the walnut a beautiful deep translucency, which will go on improving with age.

The final parting operation can be done with a skew chisel held in one hand, while the work is cradled in the other (photo 20).

A less risky procedure is to stop the lathe before the work parts company from its supporting section and trim the ends on the bandsaw, finishing them by hand.

Lever off waste wood

Gently lever off the front and back plates of waste wood so that you don't damage the walnut frame (photo 21). The glue and newspaper joint should break through fairly easily and the surfaces can be scraped clean with a cabinet scraper.

Mark the centres of each sphere for the cavity for the mechanisms and drill out the appropriate-size hole on the drill press, making sure that the work is firmly cramped down first (photos 22–24). After fitting the barometer, hygrometer and thermometer mechanisms, it's then just a matter of fixing a small brass hanging plate on the back of the finished frame and finding a suitable place to hang it. ■

Lighting-up time

How to make a distinctive wall-mounted uplighter in spalted maple

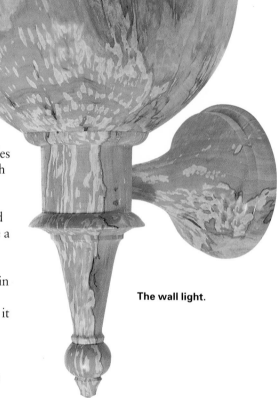

The wall light.

This wall light is made in three parts: the shade from a 100mm (4in) length of 200mm (8in) diameter log, the body from a block 160mm (6¼in) long x 80mm (3¼in) square, and the bracket from wood 100 x 100 x 100mm (4 x 4 x 4in).

To make the body, drill the hole which will house the spout of the wall-light bracket first, before turning the square block to a cylinder (photo 1). Mark a centre line along one side of the block, clamp it securely in place, and drill the hole through the line about 40mm (1⁹⁄₁₆in) from the end. Whatever means you have to drill the hole, whether by eye or, as in this case, on the drill press, you must ensure the hole is at right angles to the workpiece and passes through the central axis of the block.

Mount it between centres and tighten the tailstock, so that it's held securely. Spalted timber tends to be a bit mushy, so test its tightness on the lathe by locking the headstock spindle and twisting the workpiece in your hand. If it turns round or becomes dislodged from its centres, it will need a few more turns of the tailstock hand wheel.

To make it easier to re-centre the work, if at any stage it does become dislodged, mark the end of the workpiece with a small dot or cross corresponding to the position of the drive centre's grub screw or other reference point.

Adjust the toolrest so it runs parallel with the edge of the work, about 13mm (½in) below the height of the workpiece's centre, and set the speed to about 2000 rpm. Turn the work by hand to test that the corners of the block won't hit the toolrest when the lathe is switched on, and check that toolrest levers and tailstock barrel locks are tight.

Before starting to turn, be aware that the hole drilled in the side of the work is a cause for concern, especially if you've developed the dangerous habit of using your hand to check the roundness or to slow the work after

Photo 1 **Drilling a hole in the side of the block.**

Photo 2 **Turning the work to a cylinder.**

Photo 3 **Forming the waist section of the body of the lamp.**

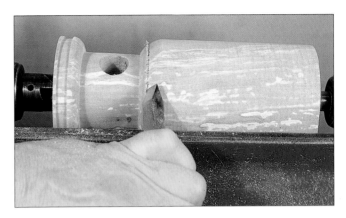

Photo 4 **Slicing the half-round moulding with the beading and parting tool.**

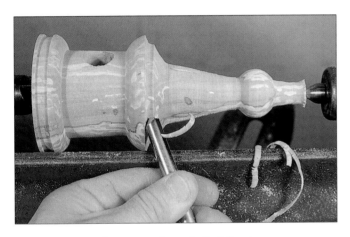

Photo 5 **Forming the concave lower half of the shape.**

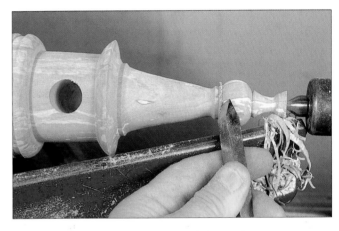

Photo 6 **Forming the ball on the end of the pendant.**

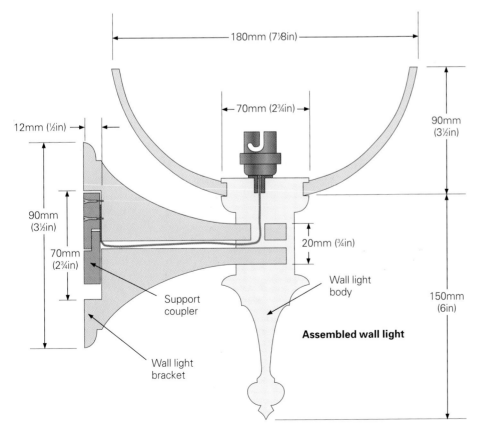

180mm (7⅛in)

70mm (2¾in)

12mm (½in)

90mm (3½in)

90mm (3½in)

70mm (2¾in)

20mm (¾in)

150mm (6in)

Support coupler

Wall light body

Assembled wall light

Wall light bracket

switching off the lathe. To avoid injuring your fingers, seal it up with a bung made from scrap wood.

Turn the work to a cylinder with a well-sharpened 19mm (¾in) roughing gouge, using the straight edge of the toolrest as a guide to run your knuckles against (photo 2). Square off one end of the cylinder by parting down with a standard 3mm (⅛in) parting tool and, using the same technique, form the joint for the shade at the top of the body. This joint takes the form of a shallow, square-cornered recess, about 1mm deep by 10mm wide (³⁄₆₄ x ⅜in), and is intended to hold the wall light's shade.

Form the cylindrical waist section of the wall-light body by parting down with the beading and parting tool (photo 3). Use the same tool to round the corners of the square sections at each end of the waist (photo 4).

This is done with the corner of the cutting edge and a twist of the handle, exactly as if you were making the side of a bead. The lower half of the body is in the shape of a tapered pendant, made roughly to shape with a 6mm (¼in) bowl gouge (photo 5).

The gouge is presented on its side and the edge held at a diagonal cutting angle, enabling it to slice through the roots of the fibres like a knife. A slice-cutting technique is essential. Spalted wood is too coarse and fibrous to be worked in any other way.

Use the beading tool again to finish the ball at the base of the pendant (photo 6). By twisting the tool onto its side at the completion of the cut, you obtain the sharp inside corner where the curve of the ball intersects the small flat steps at the top and bottom of it. These fillets, as they are called, are also the work of the beading tool.

The one at the top of the ball is the result of allowing a flat section to remain at the side of the small concave radius, formed with the small gouge, which merges with the main taper. The lower fillet is simply the left-over side of a V-cut, which could be made with the skew chisel, but in this case was sliced with the corner of the beading tool.

After sanding and polishing, part off the body section with a skew chisel held in one hand, while cradling the workpiece in the other (photo 7).

A hole is needed for the flex to pass down the centre of the body. This can be drilled by hand, with the work held in the cushioned jaws of the bench vice.

The wall bracket

Reduce the block for the bracket to a cylinder and prepare one end with a dovetail spigot, so the work can be held in a chuck. With the work gripped in the jaws, slice the free end square and flat with the 6mm (¼in) bowl gouge (photo 8).

Then cut a 13mm (½in) deep by 70mm (2¾in) diameter recess for the electrical plug and socket, using the beading and parting tool (photo 9). Drill a 6mm (¼in) hole for the flex, right through the centre of the bracket, using a drill held in the tailstock (photo 10).

Form the decorative ovolo moulding on the bracket rim next, by parting in with the beading and parting tool, so that a 13 by 13mm (½ x ½in) section remains on the edge. Then round the corner, using the standard bead-forming technique.

To make the bracket's tapered spout, part down at the end nearest the chuck, leaving enough material to support the work, and turn away

Photo 7 **Slicing off the work with the skew chisel.**

Photo 8 **Slicing the end of the bracket flat.**

Photo 9 **Cutting the recess for housing the electric coupler.**

Photo 10 **Drilling a 6mm (¼in) hole for the electric flex.**

Spalted timber

Untreated timber, if left in a damp atmosphere, will eventually begin to decay. This fungal infection produces in some woods a colourful and striking transformation called spalting.

Not all woods will spalt to the same degree, but beech, maple, London plane, sycamore and hornbeam seem to be particularly susceptible and yield some amazing effects.

You can help the process along by burying beech or maple logs in a compost heap, but leaving logs out in the rain and sun will often produce the same result. Catching the wood at the peak of the fungal attack will require cutting into the wood from time to time, to check the spread of decay – you don't want things to go too far, or you might end up with a pile of wood pulp.

Some woods spalt faster than others. Hornbeam will usually be ready after a year to 18 months, while, depending on the weather, London plane, beech and maple will take a little longer to be at their best.

Once your timber has reached the desired level of infection, bring it into the dry to prevent further fungal growth. You can convert it into smaller blocks and discs at this stage, but will need to treat the end-grain areas with wax or another form of waterproof sealant, to prevent splitting.

If you intend to make bowls, this is the time to convert the timber into rough-turned bowl blanks. Leave the sides and floor of the bowls at least 25mm (1in) thick and store in a cardboard box, or wrap them in newspaper until dry. You can, of course, make turned items from wet, unseasoned timber. Hollowed table lamps, bowls and boxes can all be turned green, so long as you are prepared for a few failures if the work cracks as it dries. Sealing the surfaces thoroughly with polish is usually adequate to prevent most of these problems.

As spalted wood contains potentially harmful fungal spores, it's essential to wear a dust mask when turning it.

Photo 11 **Forming the taper of the bracket.**

Photo 12 **Tightening the work in the chuck.**

Photo 13 **Starting the ring-tool cut.**

Photo 14 **Coming to the end of the swing.**

the bulk of the waste with a large gouge (photo 11).

The narrow end of the spout is sized to fit the hole in the lamp body by careful measuring with vernier callipers. After sanding and polishing, the bracket is parted off with the parting tool. A final hole must be drilled after the spout has been pushed home into the lamp body and glued, to let the flex pass from the centre hole in the spout up through the hole in the body.

The shade

This was made from a short length of spalted log, which, being slightly unseasoned, will shrink during the final stage of drying out. Turn this to advantage, by making the shade so that it shrinks into the recess on the head of the lamp body, creating a tight joint without the need for glue.

When mounting the log on the lathe, use the natural heart as the centre, so that any heart splits and pith can be removed when the hole for the body of the lamp is cut out.

Turn the cylinder to the desired width of the shade and prepare the work for your chuck. To provide a stronger grip than the standard chuck, I used the Masterchuck, fitted with the 75mm (3in) extension jaws (photo 12). These form a greater area of contact on a larger wooden dovetail, which is needed with low-density wood like this, as it's prone to crush under compression.

Hollowing

Flatten the end of the workpiece by slicing across with a bowl gouge held on its side with the bevel floating on the freshly exposed surface like a plane. Because of its crumbly texture,

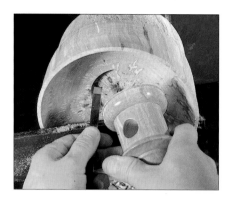

Photo 15 **Cutting the hole in the base of the shade for the body.**

Photo 16 **Preliminary parting-in cut.**

Photo 17 **Shaping the outside of the shade.**

Photo 18 **The socket fitting fits neatly out of view in the base recess of the lamp bracket.**

end grain of spalted wood is one of the most difficult materials to hollow and achieve anything like a smooth finish. As you are unlikely to get a satisfactory result with a round-nosed scraper, even with the lathe running at a faster speed, it leaves the ring tool as the obvious choice. This works like a short section of gouge which has been set at right angles to the handle.

Position the height of the toolrest so that the centre of the ring is next to the centre of the work when the tool shaft is held horizontally.

Start hollowing by resting the 90° bevel of the ring tool flat against the work surface, with the cutting edge held diagonally across the centre point of the workpiece. Start by angling the edge of the tool slightly, so that it scoops away the centre area, leaving a small depression. The tool edge is then pivoted sideways, using the toolrest as the centre of rotation. Always keep the bevel flat against the surface just cut (photos 13 and 14).

Remove swarf

As you go deeper, you may have to un-clog the ring now and then to remove swarf from the cavity wall. But always stop the lathe before putting your hand inside the hollow.

At first you can take quite heavy cuts with the ring tool, but finer ones will produce a finer finish, and put less pressure on the tool head. As you go deeper, you will need to adjust the end of the toolrest inside the opening to provide extra support.

For cavities of 75mm (3in) or more I find it helpful to fit my ring tool with a longer handle. This gives me more leverage and control when working at full stretch over the toolrest. Cut the hole in the bottom of the shade, through which the top of the lamp's body passes (photo 15), before shaping the outside. Mark a line round the work corresponding to the depth of the cavity. Leave enough space on one side of the line for the thickness of the shade and with a parting tool cut at right angles

through the body of the work (photo 16). This parting cut helps you locate the position of the base of the shade and also cuts through the fibres of the workpiece, enabling the area of waste to be removed more easily.

Shape the outside of the shade with the bowl gouge, in a series of slicing cuts (photo 17). As the sides are reduced to about 10mm (⅜in), stop the lathe and check the thickness between your fingers or with callipers, between each pass, to ensure you don't remove too much wood. While the shade is attached, sand and polish.

Sanding & polishing

Start with coarse 80-grade abrasive and work through to 400 grit to remove work and coarser sanding marks. The texture of spalted timber tends to be uneven, consisting of soft areas which will sand away forming unsightly depressions, so don't sand too heavily and use sanding blocks behind your abrasive if necessary.

The wood is very absorbent, and two or three applications of cellulose sanding sealer, painted on with a brush and the surface wiped smooth with a clean cloth while wet, will probably be needed to seal the work.

The shade can now be parted off with a handsaw, followed by a trim with a knife or chisel. Those more adventurous may even want to part off with a skew chisel.

Assembly

The top of the lamp body can now be squeezed through the hole in the base of the shade and positioned in the recess. It will take a few days for it to shrink enough to grip fast.

A bulb holder is mounted inside the shade onto the top of the lamp body and wired to the plug and socket fitting, which fits neatly out of view into the base recess of the lamp bracket. This handy fitting solves in one the problem of wiring and mounting the lamp on the wall (photo 18).

Wiring accessories include an earthed bulb holder, three-core electric cable, Luminaire Support Coupler Wall Mounted LN1663, Wall Box LNI669. ■

Kingwood clock

Highly figured kingwood makes a striking feature of this miniature clock

There are times when I enjoy putting the biggest piece of wood I can find onto my lathe, picking up a bowl gouge, and making the shavings fly. But there are times when working on a small-scale project, like this miniature clock, is equally satisfying.

I used a small piece of highly figured kingwood, an exotic hardwood with a beautiful grain of contrasting colours. At first, the aged outside surface of the timber does not look promising. But once this crust of dust and oxidised wood has been cut away, the dazzling nature of the grain is revealed.

Working small scale lets you choose from a huge range of timbers, some of which can only be obtained in small dimensions. Another advantage is that you can prepare your own timber, without the need for large industrial machinery.

This clock has been designed for a traditional living room or bedroom, but it can be made in different woods and styles to suit any setting.

The conical stand is made from a block 50 x 50 x 100mm (2 x 2 x 4in) and the circular frame from a 55mm (2¼in) diameter disc 10mm (⅜in) thick.

Making the stand

Start making the stand by first ensuring that one end of the block is perfectly flat. I made a sanding disc by facing a disc of wood with abrasive and mounting it on the lathe with a faceplate. I placed a table made from three scraps of plywood onto the bed bars of the lathe to support the work at right angles to the sander.

Find the centre of the flattened block and drill a pilot hole for the screw chuck. This hole is best drilled on the drill press because, although the screw chuck will take up some irregularities, the hole must be reasonably square.

Fit your screw chuck into the main chuck jaws and, with a pass or two of the parting tool, make sure the face

The completed clock.

Checking the flatness of the end of the work.

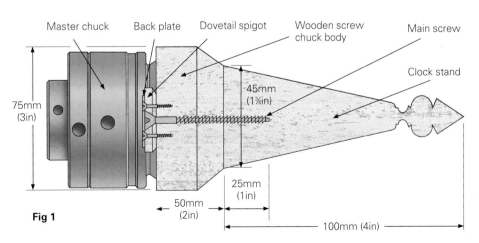

Fig 1

Master chuck · Back plate · Dovetail spigot · Wooden screw chuck body · Main screw · Clock stand

75mm (3in) · 45mm (1¾in) · 50mm (2in) · 25mm (1in) · 100mm (4in)

Fitting the work onto the chuck.

Roughing out the cone shape of the stand.

Slicing the V-cuts.

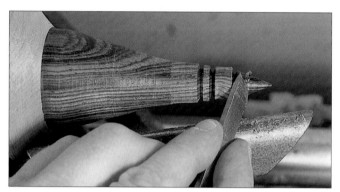
Forming the conical point of the finial.

of the wooden chuck is true and flat. Screw the block to the screw chuck until the work face comes up tight against the face of the chuck.

With the lathe speed set at about 2000rpm, use a small bowl gouge to turn the block roughly conical. You can use the revolving tail centre at this stage to provide some extra support, but you will need to ensure it does not force the end of the workpiece off the centre created by the screw chuck.

Decorative finial

To form the decorative finial at the top of the cone, you first need to make a series of V-cuts. Bring the small toolrest as close as possible to the side of the workpiece and slice into the surface with a small skew chisel.

This must be sharp if you are to obtain the desired crispness of detail. Use it with the blade almost vertical, with the longest side lying on the toolrest. Bring the tool into contact with the work so that the point of the tool penetrates the fibres cleanly at an angle, first one side of the line and then the other.

In this way the grain fibres are cut

through at their roots and the waste to one side of the cut will come away freely. To help you get the right angle, think of the swing a lumberjack uses when axing a tree.

The skew chisel is ideal for forming a conical point on top of the finial, because it slices at an angle and exerts less side pressure on the workpiece. Raise the toolrest so that the skew chisel is almost horizontal and cutting on the apex of the cone, and present the edge diagonally across the top of the workpiece at a skew – hence the name.

Lift the handle and slowly engage the edge of the tool, so that fine shavings begin to appear. To reduce the risk of the tool twisting, use only the lower half of the cutting edge, as this lies directly adjacent to the support of the toolrest. This technique produces a perfectly smooth, planed finish, and it also burnishes the surface of the work at the same time, providing a free polish.

I have had good results using the standard 3mm (⅛in) parting tool to form beads instead of the beading and parting tool. I find the cutting edge of

the tool, as it travels in an arc when the tool is twisted against the toolrest, is just at the right point to create the profile of a ball almost automatically. You only use the corner of the cutting edge anyway, so it doesn't matter how wide the tool is, and if you do slip, the parting tool usually does less damage than the 6mm (¼in) beading tool.

I used a 6mm (¼in) spindle gouge, ground with a long nose, to form the concave hollow or scotia below the bead of the finial. Each side of the hollow is cut separately.

Concave hollow

Start at the edge of the work with the gouge on its side and as it slices into the work surface, twist it so the flute pans out at the floor of the hollow. Use the parting tool again to form the small radius of the ovolo at the apex of the cone, in the same way as for the bead. This completes the finial mouldings of the stand.

To make the cone, I run a 10mm (⅜in) beading tool backwards and forwards along the toolrest, so that the corners of the edge gradually iron out the undulations and make

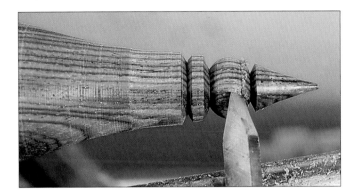

Forming the bead.

Forming the scotia.

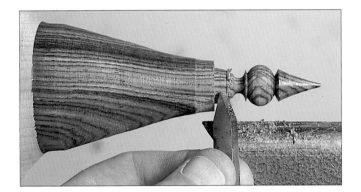

Rounding off the ovolo.

Checking the flatness of the sides.

perfectly straight sides. A short straightedge is used to continually check progress, and I even resort to a block and sandpaper to obtain the last word in flatness.

Sanding & polishing

Sanding is essential to bring out the full beauty of the grain. It's not just to smooth the work surface, but to remove tool marks. With a fine-grain wood like kingwood you needn't start with anything coarser than 250 grade, finishing with 600 grade. Cut the abrasive into small pieces and roll them up so you can get into the coves and over beads without losing the crispness of the detail.

Wipe the surface clean and apply polish with the lathe stopped. I've used a couple of coats of French polish, which is quite adequate to seal the wood when it is so tight-grained.

A clean, soft cotton cloth is best to wipe the polish into the crevices of the fine detail. After about 10 minutes the surface is dry enough to be waxed.

Carnauba wax creates one of the brightest and most durable finishes, although it is not resistant to water.

Polishing with carnauba wax.

Rub the surface all over with the carnauba stick and burnish into the work with the cloth, so it melts and spreads evenly all over. Apply the wax stick again and burnish this layer of wax with much less pressure from the cloth, so that the work is brought to an even shine.

To protect your polished tops from being scratched by the underside of the clock stand and to cover the screw hole, apply a piece of self-adhesive

baize. You can make a very neat job of trimming this by using a piece of clean 240-grade abrasive wiped across the sharp edge of the stand's base so the baize is cut.

Clock frame

To make the clock frame, drill through the centre of your blank to form a pilot hole for the screw chuck. Mount the screw chuck with 6mm (¼in) of screw protrusion into the

Screw chucks

Screw chucks are a quick and convenient way of holding work on the lathe. All you do is make sure the end of the workpiece is flat, provide a pilot hole for the screw to enter, give the piece a few twists to bring it tight against the chuck face, and away you go.

You can later re-use these wooden chucks for similar projects by providing the back of the chuck with a re-centring facility. This can be a recess cut in the back of the chuck body which centres and relocates it onto a faceplate, or you can use the method I describe here – to make a dovetail spigot on the back of the chuck which is then held in a four-jaw metal chuck.

To work properly, the screw chuck must have the screw running through the axis of the chuck body, so the first thing to do is to drill a pilot hole through a block of beech, Canadian maple or a similar hardwood.

De-grease and apply a coat of epoxy glue to the thread of a suitable screw and screw this through the block until it emerges at the end of the pilot hole. I usually use No.8 or 10 size Spax screws, precision machined from hardened steel with serrated threads which cut into most woods without the need for pre-drilling.

The pilot hole should not be so small that it extrudes the epoxy glue as the screw passes through the hole. The glue is usually sufficient to hold the screw in place, but to avoid any problems make a small back plate from a scrap of metal sheet which can be screwed over the head of the main screw.

To hold the block on the lathe while you shape the screw chuck body, use a Pozi-drive bit held in a Jacobs chuck, fitted into the lathe headstock, and hold the other end in a female centre supported in the tailstock.

I made my female centre out of a defunct dead centre, the face of which was filed flat and centre-punched. With the block held between centres in this way, turn it to a cylinder, part down at one end and form a dovetail spigot, using the parting tool on its side.

Screwing the screw through the chuck blank.

Screw chucks, tools and callipers.

Forming the dovetail on the chuck.

Screwing on the back plate.

The size and shape of the chuck will vary according to the kind of job in hand. The standard cone shape is made with tapering sides and allows the toolrest to be set right up close, giving excellent access for the turning, sanding and polishing stages.

By making the face of the chuck wide and having a very short amount of screw protruding, very shallow discs like the miniature clock frame shown can be held.

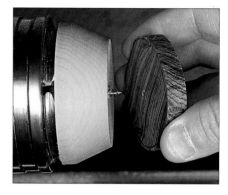
Fitting the disc for the frame onto the screw chuck.

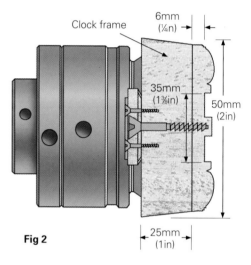

Clock frame · 6mm (¼in) · 35mm (1⅜in) · 50mm (2in) · 25mm (1in)

Fig 2

four-jaw chuck and, after checking that the face of the screw chuck is flat and running true, screw on the frame blank.

Trim the edge of the frame so it runs true, using a 6mm (¼in) bowl gouge. Direct the gouge to the centre of the rim and reverse the cut from the other side so you don't break off the corners of the disc. By slicing from each side in this way, you cut through the base of the wood fibres and get a clean finish on the rim.

I use a parting cut to flatten off the back of a small disc like this. Make sure that the parting tool is extra-sharp by honing it on the slipstone beforehand, and feed it slowly across the disc, taking off no more than a millimetre's width of cut at a time.

Check that the frame lies flat against the clock stand before sanding and sealing. After unwinding, reverse the frame and remount it onto the screw chuck. It should self-centre on the screw, but if not, you may need to trim the rim a little more.

Hollowing the recess for the clock mechanism is best done with a square-ended scraper which has had its sides ground back so they don't bind against the recess wall. Leave a small area on each side of the screw so that the strength of the chuck's grip is not reduced, and cut to the full depth of the mechanism by feeding the scraper in at a standard horizontal angle.

Check the depth with a depth gauge and then take similar cuts, working towards the outside of the recess. You can use a pair of vernier callipers to make sure you don't get the recess too wide, but the final test is pressing in the clock mechanism. This is fitted with a soft, spongy nylon ring which compresses and keeps the mechanism in place.

The frame's small, round moulding is formed by re-setting the toolrest at a 45° angle and gently slicing away the corner with a lateral movement of a freshly sharpened parting tool, using only the corner to cut.

Don't try to roll the tool on its side because this will probably cause the edge to dig in, due to the direction of the grain fibres, which does not allow them to be cut off cleanly.

Parting cut

Using a simple parting-cut technique to do the shaping works nearly as well, especially with tight-grained wood, but with this method you will be relying entirely on the razor sharpness of the tool edge.

After sanding and polishing the frame, trim off the bit of waste in the centre of the recess with a chisel, and countersink the hole for the small wood screw which will attach the frame to the stand.

Position the frame against the side of the stand and mark through the hole with a bradawl. The screw chuck makes a handy holding device when drilling the pilot hole. With dense hardwoods like kingwood, it's essential to get the hole the correct size. There is nothing more irritating than to get to the final assembly stage and strip the screw because the pilot hole is too small. Do a trial run with a scrap of the same wood to avoid any hitch on the real thing. ■

Trimming the edge of the clock frame.

Flattening off the back face of the frame.

Checking the width of the recess for the clock.

Forming the torus shape on the edge of the frame.

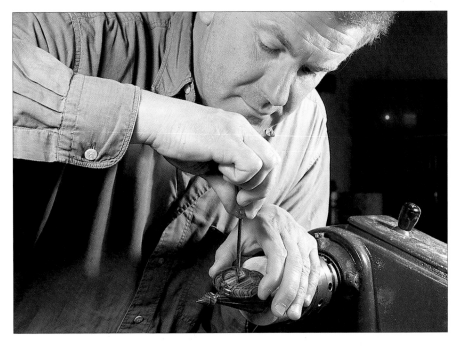
Screwing the clock frame to the stand.

Thread care

The completed sewing stand.

This graceful sewing stand in box and pear is joined together by a fine screw thread

Screw threads add an extra dimension to any turning. I've included a threaded joint in this cotton-reel and pincushion stand. You will need thread-chasing tools to make it. These come in sets of two – one for internal threads, and the other for external. They vary in the number of teeth per inch, but one of the most useful sizes for small turned projects is a BSW 16 to the inch.

To include a fine-threaded joint in your stand you will need an exceptionally close-grained wood, such as boxwood, lignum vitae, or a fine-textured rosewood. Even if you do cut a section of clean thread on a piece of more fibrous wood, it may crumble during use.

Practice is needed before you can chase threads with confidence. I have a collection of chewed-up noggins to prove it. To have any chance of thread-chasing success, you should practice on prize pieces of boxwood. Coarser-grained wood will not do.

The biggest aid to thread cutting is to develop a smooth, gentle cutting action. It helps to complete the cutting before you spend a lot of time on the rest of the project. This way you have the full diameter of the blank to play with, so that if you

mess up your first internal thread, you can try again. If necessary, you can modify the stem shape to take the increased width of the central threaded hole.

Internal thread

Drill a hole 19mm diameter by 19mm deep (¾ x ¾in) in the block for the base of the stand, using a saw-tooth centre drill. Cut a 5mm (³⁄₁₆in) long rebate into the side of the wall at the bottom of the hole, using the side-cutting scraper (photo 1). It makes a space into which the thread chaser can work at the completion of its thread-cutting run.

This space is vital, for without it

Photo 1 **Side-rebating the bottom of the hole.**

the front of the cutter would hit the bottom of the hole and mince the threads. Round the edge of the hole, at the entrance, with a scraper, forming a curved bevel. It's needed for the first stages of thread cutting. Set the lathe speed to about 200rpm and adjust the toolrest, so that when the thread chaser is held horizontally, the teeth are 2–3mm above the lathe centre. Make sure the top of the toolrest and the underside of the chaser are perfectly clean and smooth, and apply a little candle wax or grease to lubricate the surfaces.

To start the thread, hold the chaser at 45° and

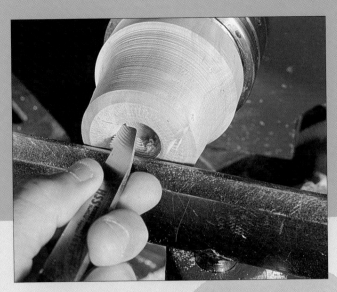

Photo 2 **Forming the internal thread with the thread chaser.**

Photo 3 **Cutting a space for the chaser to work into.**

feed it forward, gently brushing the corner of the opening. As soon as the teeth begin to form a thread and tug the tool forward, let the tool draw itself along.

Before taking the thread on the corner to its final depth, stop the lathe and check you are forming a single thread and not a double or triple. This happens if your initial feeding of the tool is too quick.

To continue the thread round the corner and down the side of the hole, gently swing the chaser tool in a horizontal arc, using just enough lateral pressure to hold it in the corner thread. Allow the thread to draw the tool freely, gradually increasing the length of the section of thread down the side of the hole. But flick the cutter out of the threads before it hits the bottom of the hole.

Work the section to be threaded lightly at first, along its length, and gradually take the thread to its full depth by repeated passes with the chaser (photo 2). Get to know the speed at which the tool is pulled forwards and anticipate when it reaches the end of the thread, to build a rhythm, and start cutting deeper into the thread already cut.

External thread

A dowel must be formed at the end of your upper stem section which is 2mm (⁵⁄₆₄in) thicker than the inside

measurement across the threaded hole. Cut a space for the chaser to work into, using a standard parting tool (photo 3).

Before you start cutting a thread, ensure the lower corners of the chasing tool's shaft have been well rounded, so they don't bite into the top of the toolrest.

The latter should be adjusted so

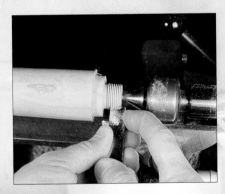

Photo 4 **Chasing a thread onto the dowel.**

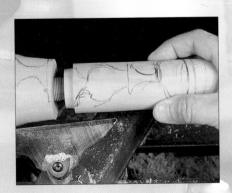

Photo 5 **Testing the screw joint.**

that the cut occurs at centre height.

The principles that applied to cutting the internal thread also apply here, but more pressure must be put on the side of the tool, to help it slide laterally along the toolrest (photo 4). Test that the two parts fit together before starting to turn the stand (photo 5).

Turning the stand

Most of the stand was turned using the spindle gouge, a tool which can form all kinds of curved shapes, as well as deep, narrow coves. I grind the bevel of new spindle gouges to a longer, more acute angle than that supplied by the manufacturer, forming the end into a lady's-fingernail shape. The tool's small cutting radius and thick shaft make it controllable even at some distance from the toolrest.

To form deep, hollow coves, start by using the gouge fairly flat and twist the point in the work surface to form a shallow depression. Slice down each side of this with the gouge on its side, rotating it so it pans out at the base of the hollow. Reduce the cut as you work further away from the toolrest, especially when making tight radiuses, where the gouge tends to snatch in the sides of the hollow.

The spindle gouge can also cut a fairly crisp V-cut, by using the point

Photo 6 **Cutting the pincushion recess in the top of the stand.**

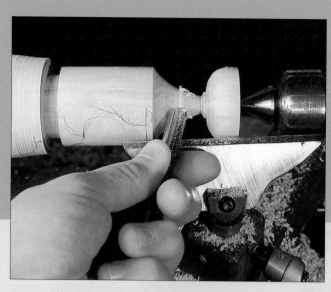

Photo 7 **Paring down at the neck of the stand to form a stem.**

to slice alternately from each side of a centre line, following the same procedure as for the skew chisel. The side-cutting edges of the gouge can then be used at an acute slicing angle to round the shoulders and form round convex shapes. To keep control, continue to gently press the bevel against the work surface, so it follows the curve.

Outer shape

The work is screwed together and supported at one end in the chuck, and at the other by the tailstock. Use the side-cutting scraper to recess the top of the stand to take the pincushion, leaving a small spigot in the centre for the revolving centre to bear upon (photo 6). Form the bowl of the pincushion with the long, fingernail point of the spindle gouge.

Work the tool on its side, so the bevel lies against the workpiece surface at all times. Then cut from the opposite direction (photo 7) and use the small radius of the point to form a V-cut at the foot of the bowl.

When the bowl has been completed, you can move on and work on the next section of the stand.

It's important not to reduce the diameter of the block nearest the chuck before completing the upper sections, or you'll weaken the

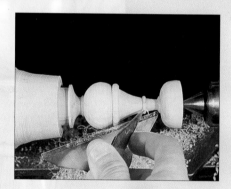

Photo 8 **Shaping the side of a bead with the parting tool.**

stability of the workpiece. The same gouge can be used to form the narrow neck below the pear shape of the top section. It will even form the

beads on the upper sides of the 'pear', although I usually complete them with a parting tool (photo 8).

Use this tool to form a parallel shoulder at the base of the top section on which the tray of the stand can locate. Form the outline of the wine-glass shape of the base section, with the spindle gouge, by first cutting a deep V-shaped crevice. I usually make a parting cut at the base of the stand at this stage, and then form the ovolo-shaped foot with a 6mm (¼in) beading and parting tool (photo 9).

The narrow waist of the vase shape, hollowed with the spindle gouge, is worked by pivoting it against a back rest, made by simply

Photo 9 **Cutting the small ovolo on the foot of the stand with a beading and parting tool.**

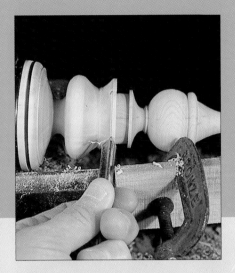

Photo 10 **Using a back rest to support the spindle gouge.**

G-cramping a slip of wood to the toolrest. This stops the gouge from slipping backwards and digging in at the start of the cut, when there is nothing to support the bevel (photo 10).

Cotton-reel tray

I used a disc of contrasting pearwood, 127mm diameter by 10mm thick (5 x ⅜in), for the tray which holds the cotton reels; the wood's pinkness was caused by steam treatment before air seasoning.

To make it, sand the disc flat and then, using double-sided carpet tape, mount it on a faceplate which has been faced with a scrapwood disc. The disc provides a soft material for the drill to pass into when the tray's centre hole is being drilled.

Tape the plate and the back of the workpiece, so both surfaces can be burnished down with the handle of a screwdriver. Squeeze the assembly together in the bench vice, to make sure the joint is secure (photo 11).

Flatten the face of the disc with a round-nosed scraper, using your knuckle against the back of the toolrest to guide the tool across in a parallel plane. Trim the outside edge of the disc with a 6mm (¼in) bowl gouge, working the tool from both sides towards the middle. In this way the square corners are preserved.

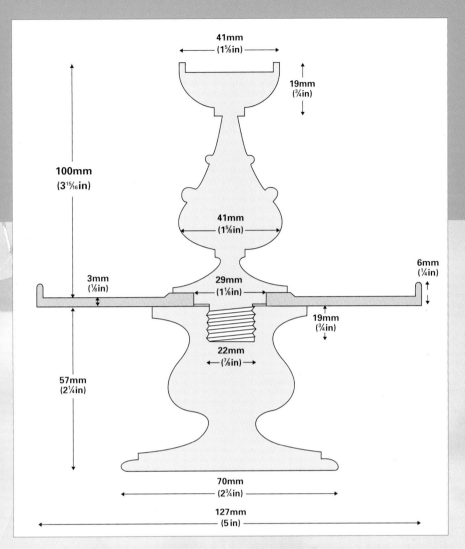

Photo 11 **Cramping the tray blank to the faceplate, using double-sided tape.**

Photo 12 **Drilling the hole through the centre of the tray.**

Photo 13: **Cutting the recess.**

Drill a 25mm (1in) hole through the tray with a saw-tooth centre drill, fitted in the tailstock (photo 12). This can be widened to accept the shoulder at the base of the stand's top section.

Cut the recess for the cotton reels with a square scraper. The contrasting pearwood I used for the tray is fairly dense, which means it will take fine detail even when scraped into shape.

Make sure your scraper is really sharp and that when you use it the toolrest is very close to the workface. To get the best finish from your scraper, use the tool in a lateral direction, with just the corner of the edge cutting (photo 13). Check there's enough space for the base of a cotton reel to fit into and that the floor of the tray is level (photo 14). Sand the work smooth and apply a suitable polish.

When prying the finished work off the lathe, don't be surprised by just how strong the bond is between your finished tray and the faceplate. Slowly apply firm, rather than heavy, pressure to the back of the work with your thumbs, so the double-sided tape has time to separate.

Sanding & polishing

With a fine-grained wood like boxwood, great care must be taken during the finishing process to make

the most of its subtle figuring. The slightest blemish left by the tool or abrasive will be more conspicuous with this timber than with the medium to coarse woods.

You probably won't need to start with an abrasive coarser than 150 grade, unless you want to shape or round the beads or the edge of the tray. Then apply 240 and 320 grade.

At this stage you will begin to see the grain appear, along with any faults. These will need sanding away with the coarser abrasive. A final application of 600 grade should ensure the only marks you see are those in the grain.

Boxwood has a very dense

texture, which needs little polish to seal. I give it a coat or two of shellac, wiped on with a soft cotton cloth, and then apply carnauba wax for a high gloss. In its pure form, carnauba comes as a hard stick, which is rubbed against the work while it rotates, melting wax over it.

Rub the wax into the grain, using a clean, soft cotton or flannelette cloth. Apply another thinner coat with the wax stick and burnish with the cloth, gradually decreasing the pressure so a fine even layer is brought to a high shine. Parting off is done with the parting tool, after unscrewing the stand's top section. ■

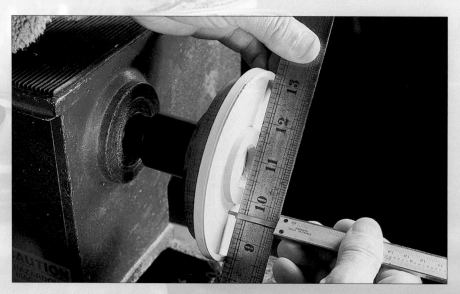

Photo 14 **Checking the depth of the recess.**

The cocobolo jewellery box.

A jewellery box made from the beautiful, but potentially hazardous wood, cocobolo

Jewel of a box

Cocobolo is a beautiful, exotic wood. But it can damage your health if inhaled over a long period, so you'll need a good-quality dust mask or respirator if you use it to make this jewellery box. You should also have an effective dust extraction system to suck the dust away. I often rig an extractor pipe to the toolrest with a strong elastic band (photo 1), which collects the ultra-fine particles that do the most harm as close to the source as possible.

Make sure your wood is completely dry, because any shrinkage in the finished workpiece will cause the gold-plated hinge encircling the lid and body to loosen. I was lucky to find a piece of snuff-dry cocobolo in a timber yard's pile of old leftover stock. It had lain there for more than 50 years.

Although cocobolo is a little bit on the oily side, it turns well, and its dense texture makes it good for fine detail, while the striking colour and richly figured grain produces a dazzling effect when polished.

The box's lid and base are constructed so that the striped figure of the grain runs continuously through the workpiece. To achieve this decorative effect, first saw the cocobolo block into two halves on the bandsaw and mount each piece in turn firmly between centres, so the square corners can be cut away with a roughing gouge.

Take each block and on the opposite end to the freshly sawn end, part down with a beading and parting tool to form a 6mm (¼in) long dovetail spigot, the correct diameter to fit into your chuck. Cut the dovetail with the beading tool laid flat on its side on the toolrest, so the top edge of the diamond tip scrapes into the corner of the shoulder (photo 2).

Making the body

With the block for the box's body mounted firmly in your chuck jaws, set the toolrest diagonally across the corner and slice the end flat, using a small 6mm (¼in) bowl gouge. Start the cut slowly with the gouge on its side and anchored down on the toolrest so it can't snatch into the corner of the cylinder.

Slowly edge the gouge forward with the bevel in line with the cut. Once you have traversed the exposed corner and cut a little way across the face, the gouge's bevel will be supported by the freshly cut surface, so you can relax your grip slightly and allow the tool to cut at its own speed (photo 3).

Form a tightly fitting rebate for the hinge on the corner of the base with the beading tool, using a simple

PHOTO 1 **Extractor rigged up to collect dust**.

PHOTO 3 **Slicing off the face of the block with the 6mm (¼in) bowl gouge.**

PHOTO 2 **Forming the dovetail in the spigot with the beading tool on its side.**

The astragal's bead is rounded by gently nibbling at the corners of the square section with the freshly sharpened beading tool. Keep the tool at a cutting angle to the work but maintain the edge in a horizontal plane when cutting each shallow facet. Even though the wood has a fairly cheesy texture, the edge of your beading tool will need to be freshly sharpened to obtain a crisp, clean finish.

The conventional lateral rolling technique of forming beads, which produces an even cleaner finish, is more difficult to master, and not absolutely necessary when working in these fine-textured woods.

Forming the small concave radius in the top edge of the plinth is done with a similar technique, using the point of a sharply rounded spindle gouge. Put the gouge on the toolrest and arc the handle so the tool cuts in the direction of the grain. With each pass of the tool the point must be held at a very shallow depth of cut so it does not catch in the hard fibres of the end grain.

parting cut. Mark out the design of the box on the side and use the same parting cut technique to form steps and square sections which will form the outer perimeters of the astragal, the plinth and the slightly tapered middle area of the box (photo 4).

PHOTO 4 **Blocking out the shape of the outside of the box.**

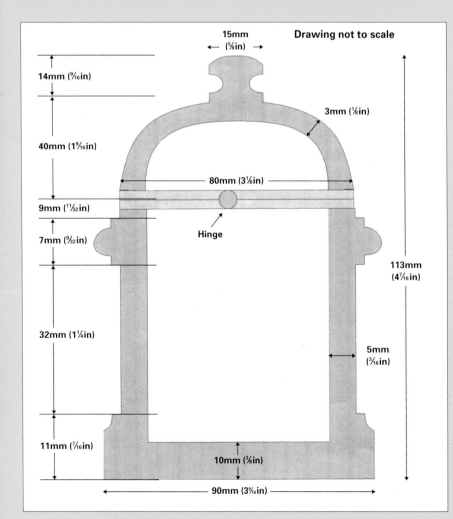

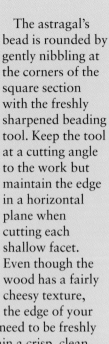

15mm (⅝in)

Drawing not to scale

14mm (⁹⁄₁₆in)

40mm (1⁹⁄₁₆in)

3mm (⅛in)

80mm (3⅛in)

9mm (¹¹⁄₃₂in)

Hinge

7mm (⁹⁄₃₂in)

32mm (1¼in)

113mm (4⁷⁄₁₆in)

5mm (³⁄₁₆in)

11mm (⁷⁄₁₆in)

10mm (⅜in)

90mm (3⁹⁄₁₆in)

To clean up the straight, tapered sides of the box, use a lateral cutting technique with the beading tool. This involves placing the edge of the tool on the apex of the work so it's only just cutting, then slowly feeding the tool sideways, using the corner of the edge to cut.

In this way the uneven surfaces are flattened and a smooth, flattened surface goes right into the corners next to the mouldings. Use the same technique to reduce the shoulder nearest the hinge, to make it flush with the outer surface of the ring hinge.

PHOTO 5 **A longer handle adds leverage and support for the cut when at full stretch.**

Hollowing the box

Use a combination of round and square scrapers for this job. Most woodturners use their scrapers straight from the dry grindstone, having created a substantial bur on the edge first. For the best results on a wet stone, I grind a much longer bevel and hone it until I achieve a chisel-sharp edge, which will stand repeated honings before it needs another grinding.

I also fit a longer handle to add leverage and support for the cut when at full stretch (photo 5). Make a deep excavation in the centre of the box first with a 13mm (½in) round scraper, preferably ground with a sharp hair-pin curve.

Start the cut in the middle of the workface and work towards the edge of the box by slowly swinging the handle in a horizontal arc. You can remove almost all the waste material in this way before turning to the square scraper to form the square corners of the cavity.

For forming the deep square

PHOTO 6 **Reaming down the wall of the box.**

corners of a box, I use a 25mm (1in) square-end scraper which has had its side edge ground back (photo 6). This prevents it binding against the concave surface it's working against. The tool is used in a forward motion to remove most of the waste, straight into the face of the work.

Slide the corner of the scraper into the curved surface produced by the round scraper and stop when the cut becomes too wide to control. This will create a succession of steps which can then be removed more safely by a lateral cut of the tool.

Place the sharpened side edge of the scraper about 1mm (³⁄₆₄in) in from the top of the nearest step and slowly feed the tool sideways, until it brushes lightly against the wall of the box. The bottom is cleaned up in the same way, by starting the cut in the centre with the scraper at a slight angle, so its trailing edge rides clear of the floor.

The full width of the cutting edge must be prevented from biting into the box floor at all costs, as this will cause a tremendous snatch and may dislodge the workpiece. A final forward reaming cut directed down the side of the box is then all that's necessary to clean up the inside wall.

Sanding

With a fine-grained wood I start with 240 grit, work my way through 320 and end with 600 grit. Each successive grade should remove the scratch marks of the previous grade, but if when you get to the finer grades you find a blemish stubbornly refuses to budge, you will need to go back over your work again with a slightly coarser-grit abrasive.

When the surface is perfectly smooth and free from any marks other than

the wood's grain, it can be sealed with polish. For a wood as beautiful as cocobolo, only the very best finish will do. I use traditional French polish, wiped on with the lathe stationary, using a piece of clean cotton flannelette.

A layer of pure carnauba wax is then applied by holding the stick against the revolving work, which causes the wax to melt. This is burnished with a new piece of soft cotton cloth to a smooth, even shine.

To get to the base, to remove the spigot and sand and polish the bottom of the box, remove the workpiece from the chuck. Jam-fit it onto a mandrel made from a piece of waste wood held on a faceplate.

You will need to take great care over the sizing of this mandrel so that the grip is tight enough to hold the work but not so tight that it splits the box. You can also bring the revolving centre of the tailstock up to support the workpiece while you slice the bottom clean with the small bowl gouge, until just the central pip has to be removed.

Making the lid

Mount the block for the lid on the chuck and cut a rebate for the gold hinge in the same way as you did for the base. Use a ring tool to hollow the lid and produce a cleaner finish than can you can usually get with a scraper. This slices through the end fibres at a more acute angle and has the extra advantage that it exerts least leverage on the workpiece.

Prepare the face by flattening it with the small gouge to get it true and smooth. Adjust the height of the toolrest so that the centre of the ring tool, held horizontally, is diagonally across the centre of the workpiece.

Start the cut by angling the edge of the tool slightly so it scoops away the central area, leaving a small depression. Slowly gyrate the tool, using the toolrest as the centre of rotation and keeping the bevel flat with the concave surface of the hollow.

You should soon create a continuous flow of fine spiral

PHOTO 7 **Hollowing the lid with the ring tool.**

PHOTO 8 **Forming the dome of the lid with the 6mm (¼in) bowl gouge.**

PHOTO 9 **Forming the scotia moulding of the knob.**

shavings – a sign that the tool is cutting correctly (photo 7). You can take quite heavy cuts at first, but as you work further from the toolrest's support you need to limit the depth of cut.

To enable the tool to cut cleanly, keep the ring clear of shavings after each cut and remove the swarf, which may build up against the walls of the cavity. Remember, before you put your fingers into the opening to clear shavings, switch off the lathe and wait for the work to come to rest.

After hollowing out, use the small gouge to start shaping the outside of the lid while it is held in the chuck. Doing some of the work while it is set up in this way allows you to feel the thickness of the lid between your fingers as it is developing.

To finish off the lid, use the same chucking technique as you did for the body of the box by carefully jam-fitting the lid onto a wooden mandrel. Bring the toolrest as close as you can to the workpiece and continue forming the dome of the lid with the bowl gouge. Leave a small spigot section for the knob or finial (photo 8).

PHOTO 10 **Burnishing the lid to a high gloss.**

This is then shaped with the long-nosed spindle gouge by first undercutting at the base of the knob to form a small cove or scotia moulding. To do this, use the point of the gouge on its side and twist the tool round as it cuts, bringing it to a level position as it reaches the base of the cove. Repeat this mirror-fashion to produce the other side, so that the two sides are symmetrical (photo 9).

After slicing the top of the knob smooth to produce a slight dome with the bowl gouge, form a tiny fillet with the corner of the beading tool to articulate the convex dome of the lid and the concave hollow of the knob.

When sanding the lid, don't be tempted to use blunt abrasive, as this will just burnish the wood and sometimes the heat build-up will cause fine end-grain cracking. This can spoil an otherwise perfect piece of turned work. Once sanded, finish using the method and materials described previously (photo10). Glue the hinge firmly in place with some epoxy glue. ■

The completed box.

Three-point turn

An elegant tripod table, based on part of a 17th-century design

Tripod table, based on an old design.

I drew inspiration for my tripod table from a four-legged, 17th-century oak side table, because its legs were more refined than those of the cruder three-legged versions made in the past. If you reproduce an old piece of furniture, you don't have to stick to the original shape – you might want to remove a bead or fussy piece of decoration, or add some extra detail. But you must pay attention to the proportions and balance of the piece, as well as to practicalities such as providing structural strength where it's needed.

Tripod tables were made from almost any English hardwood, different species often being used for each part of the construction. I'm using elm, a traditional timber for furniture making. Elm must be well seasoned, as it's prone to warp when green.

You will need a disc, 300mm diameter x 18mm thick (11¾ x ¾in), for the top; a block, 70 x 70 x 480mm (2¾ x 2¾ x 19in), for the central stem; and three blocks, 45 x 45 x 175mm (1¾ x 1¾ x 7in), for the legs.

Marking out

Mark the centres at each end of the wood for the table stem and fix it between centres. Set the lathe speed to about 2000rpm and turn the square block to a 70mm (2¾in) diameter cylinder, using a large roughing gouge. Leave a 60mm

(2⅜in) long section at the end nearest the tailstock and part down with a parting tool to form a square shoulder and reduce the rest of the spindle to 500mm (19¾in).

To copy the lateral dimensions of the turned work from the pattern leg, take a straight strip of wood and G-cramp it to the side of the leg. Place a try square against the rod so that it spans across and intersects each of the mouldings' junction points. You can then draw a

Photo 1 **Late 17th-century oak side table from which the table stem was copied.**

Photo 2 **Taking the lateral dimensions off the leg.**

Photo 3 **Reducing the top of the spindle to steps and square sections**.

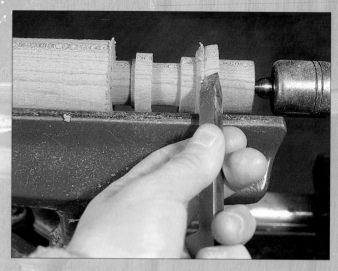

Photo 4 **Forming the ovolo at the top of the stem**.

corresponding line on the rod which can then be laid against the side of the workpiece and the marked-out positions drawn round the spindle as rings.

If possible, mount the original leg above the workpiece, so that you can constantly refer back to it as you work. A quick glance to check the original shape before you make a cut will often prevent you removing waste from the wrong side of the line; an easy mistake on a complicated set of mouldings.

Decorative mouldings

Start at the end of the table stem furthest from the headstock, so the rigidity afforded by the full width of the workpiece is prolonged until the last stages of turning. At the top of the stem use a beading and parting tool to form a dowel about 25mm long x 32mm wide (1 x 1¼in), or to any suitable width which will match a corresponding drill size. Make sure it is parallel and that the face of the shoulder is slightly undercut, to avoid a gap appearing around the edge of the joint when the dowel is pushed home.

Using callipers set to the diameters of the mouldings you are copying, cut a section of the stem down to each width, so that a series of square-sided steps are produced which correspond to the outer

perimeters of the beads, fillets and ovolos to be formed.

Round off the half-bead or ovolo at the top edge of the stem, using the corner of the beading and parting tool. To perform this cut successfully and fairly consistently, the tool must be in perfect shape; the bevels on each side of the tool should be ground long and the edge straight across, so that the corners are square.

Photo 5 **Forming the concave radius with the spindle gouge**.

Photo 6 **Round off the square sections to form beads etc**.

To complete the edge, hone it on an oilstone. Place the tool nearly flat on the work surface and twist it so that the corner makes contact and lifts the wood fibres slightly. The photo above shows the ovolo nearly fully developed, after the corner has been removed by repeated rolling cuts.

At this stage twist the beading tool onto its side, cutting the last fine shaving away with the point of the corner. At the base of the ovolo, leave a thin band or fillet about 3mm (⅛in) wide and form the concave radius which sweeps down to meet the neck of the stem using a spindle gouge. The cut is started with the tool on its side and then, with a twisting action, it is brought round to a level plane at the neck of the stem.

The same tool is used to shape the bead on the neck of the stem, and the photo shows the beading tool when it has been rolled almost right over on its side at the completion of its cut. Later, the beading tool will be in action again, shaping the bulbous part of the pear shape at the base of the stem.

Just before this, I used the beading tool on its side to form the V-cut which divides the bulb of the pear shape from the hollow cove or scotia just above. The tool is fed into the wood on its side first on one side of the V and then the other, removing a thin section of wood no more than a millimetre thick at a time.

Photo 7 **Using the beading and parting tool to slice a V-cut.**

Photo 8 **Forming the hollow curve of the pear shape at the base of the table stem.**

The gouge performs the same cut, but on the larger radius which forms part of the pear-shaped lower half of the table stem.

The long straight taper of the stem's middle section is cut with a freshly sharpened roughing gouge.

Tripod leg holes

Mark out the centres for the three splayed legs that will fit into the 70mm (2 ¾in) base section. This is a straightforward task with a dividing head, but if you don't have one you can, with some basic geometry, make a simple device that will do the same job from a piece of card.

Drilling the holes at the same angle should not be left to guesswork. I've made a very effective drilling jig out of a hardwood block. Drill a hole, the same size as the dowel you intend to use to hold the legs into the stem, squarely through the block using the drill press.

Hold the block between centres and turn a spigot which fits firmly in the toolrest banjo. To set the jig, feed the drill through the hole in the block and position it so that its point is at the same height as the lathe centre. Then set it at an angle so that there is a 30° rake on the legs.

Twist the stem round so that the three leg positions line up with the point of the drill, and drill each hole in turn. You are then free to

complete the base by rounding its underside and adding an optional small finial at the bottom.

Wear a face shield at all times when turning on the lathe, especially with thin-sectioned, wide-diameter work.

Table top

The top is made from a single piece of well-seasoned elm. It's in the form of a shallow tray, which has a D-shaped moulding decorating the surrounding rim. Plane the underside of the table top flat and screw a faceplate securely in the centre.

Take care that the screws are not too long, or they may show through when you come to hollow the middle area of the tray-shaped top. Set the lathe to about 1000rpm and trim the outer edge of the disc true, using a small 6mm (¼in) bowl gouge. Making the edge concentric requires working the gouge from each side of the disc towards the middle, so that the corners are not broken off.

Use the gouge with the bevel lined up with the cut and feed it across so that it slices through the surface, removing a thin section of wood in one steady, controlled movement. Stop the lathe after each cut to check that the disc is completely concentric, and then use the same slice-cutting technique to form a

Photo 9 **Marking out the leg centres.**

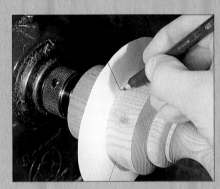

Photo 10 **Drilling the holes in the stem's base for the legs.**

Photo 11 **Cleaning the top's outer edge .**

Photo 12 **Cleaning the edge of the disc.**

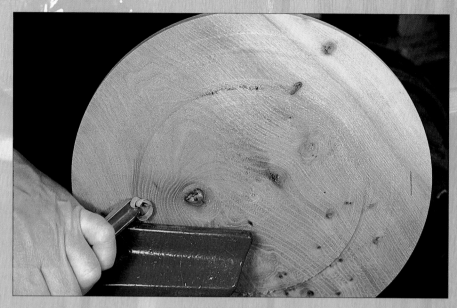

Photo 13 **Forming the section for the decorative rim of the table.**

curved chamfer on the underside corner of the rim. Flatten the face of the table top with a 10mm (⅜in) bowl gouge.

Rim moulding

Do any mouldings or decoration to the rim of the table top before hollowing the top. This is because when the thickness of the board is reduced by hollowing the central area, stresses inside the wood will be released, warping the table top. However, you will need to hollow a small area near the edge to establish the rim width. This is done with the spindle gouge.

To support the gouge and prevent it slipping back and tearing the edge of the rim, I use a vertical tool post, made from a masonry nail placed in a hole in the toolrest. To make the D-moulding, first cut two tiny rebates in each corner of the rim with a small parting tool.

By performing a gentle forward parting cut from various angles using the same tool, chip away at the corners and create a series of facets. Make sure you've made a good job of honing the parting tool beforehand, as the crispness of the moulding will depend on the sharpness of the edge. Sand the small facets with 100-grit abrasive, producing the round shape of the D-moulding. This is best done straight away while the rim is still running true.

You can now concentrate on hollowing the top with a round-nosed scraper to form the flat

Photo 14 **Cutting two rebates on each side of the section for the D-shape moulding.**

floor of the tray shape. Make light cuts with the scraper by sliding the knuckle of your forefinger against the back of the toolrest to help guide the cut. Test the surface with a straightedge and use a flat sanding block to maintain the flatness when you sand the top smooth.

Three splayed legs

The drumstick design of the three splayed legs is the simplest of shapes to make, but not the easiest to

reproduce. This is because there are very few datum points to guide you, the design being made up of nothing but three curves, which need a good eye to match accurately.

One trick I've learnt, when doing a set of duplicate turnings, is to leave the spindles with their waste ends intact until the last one has been made. It's then possible, if a mistake is made to one of the legs, to fix the others back on their centres and do any modifications required to make them match. Wear a dust mask when you sand.

Sanding & polishing

I use J-flex aluminium-oxide cloth abrasive, which works in and out of tight curves. I start with 100 grit, work my way through 240, and finish off with 400 grit, using each successive grade to remove the previous grade's scratches. When the surface is perfectly smooth and free of man-made marks, seal with some polish.

For a coarse-grained wood like elm, I use a soft, fast-drying Briwax, or its equivalent. This is rubbed on with the lathe stationary and burnished with it switched on. It gives a soft, shiny, non-heat, non-water-resistant finish. If you can put up with the odd mark or two standing out at first, it will improve with further waxing and over the years take on a deep, translucent, antique patina.

Assembly

Sophisticated methods of assembly use buttons to hold the top down, at the same time allowing for shrinkage, but I've used the traditional way of joining the top to the central stem. I glue and wedge the dowel into an intermediary block, which is then simply screwed into the underside of the table top. ∎

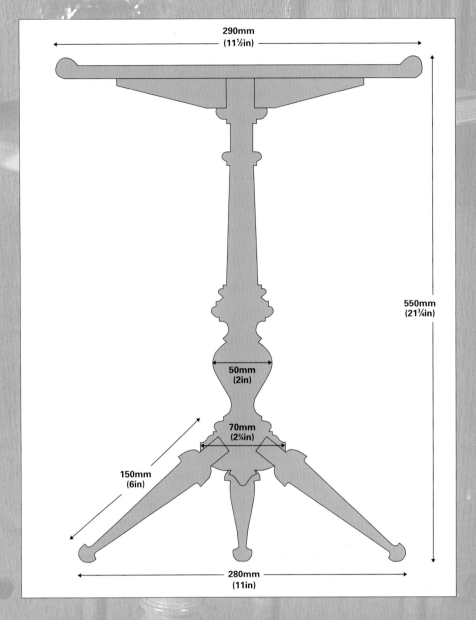

290mm (11½in)

550mm (21¾in)

50mm (2in)

70mm (2¾in)

150mm (6in)

280mm (11in)

Photo 15 **Forming the D-moulding.**

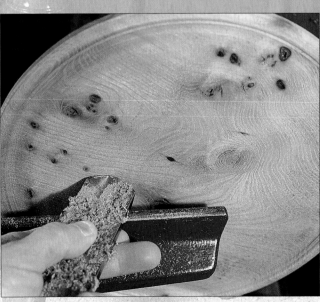

Photo 16 **Skimming the table top flat.**

Cherry 'chalice'

A large covered cup in the 17th-century style, turned from a cherry-tree butt

The completed cup.

This large covered cup was loosely based on a collection of chalices dating back to the 1600s. I'd thought, as many did, that they were used in communion services – until I read that in 1063 the Church had forbidden timber chalices on the grounds that wood 'absorbed the Host.' Or the cups may have been used as part of 17th-century societies' insignia. Whatever their original purpose, they provide an excellent opportunity to test your turning skills and to make an unusual container.

I made mine from two sections of cherry log – one 150mm (6in) long for the lid and another 200mm (8in) long for the base. They were cut from a cherry-tree butt which had been stored in a shed for two or three years to make sure it was dry enough for use.

Even so, wood this thick is never fully seasoned, so only suitable for hollow projects. If used for one where the central core is not hollowed, the difference in moisture content between the dryer heartwood and the perimeter will result in the finished workpiece splitting down the side.

A handy device can be used to find the centre at the end of the log, even when the sides are irregular. It's made by scratching a series of gradually decreasing circles into a sheet of Perspex. The circles nearest the outer edge of the log are used as a sight, while the centre is marked on the log through a hole in the middle of the target.

The ends of the log are usually full of heart shakes, so keep sawing slices of waste until you come to an area free from splits. Then cut a section for the lid, about 150–200m (6–8in) long, and mount it securely on the lathe, between centres.

Set the lathe speed to about 500rpm and turn away the bark and outer surface of the log with a roughing gouge until you have balanced the work and formed a smooth cylinder. Use a parting tool to flatten off one end of the cylinder, leaving a small spigot at the centre to centrally locate the faceplate.

I use four 30mm (1⅛in) long Spax – hardened steel screws – to attach the faceplate. These have serrated threads which screw straight into the hardest of woods,

Photo 1 Slicing the end of the log with a 10mm (⅜in) bowl gouge.

Photo 2 Reverse the ring tool to cut the walls with the 45° edge.

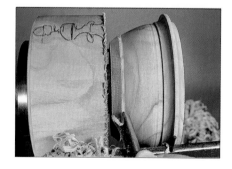

Photo 3 Cutting the dome of the lid by slicing with a gouge.

Photo 4 Jam-fitting the lid onto the spigot.

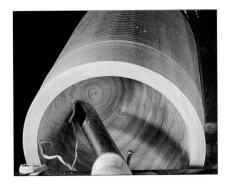

Photo 6 Hollowing the inside of the chalice with the Supertip hollowing tool.

without need for pre-drilling.

The other method for holding the work is to use a compression chuck. This has the advantage that it does not leave screw holes, but the faceplate will hold the work more closely to the headstock than a chuck. This reduced overhang means the workpiece is much steadier, allowing heavier cuts to be taken.

With the work mounted on the lathe at one end, prepare the other end for hollowing by slicing it clean and true with a small bowl gouge. You can see the action of the gouge in close-up in photo 1 as it slices across the end of the cylinder with its bevel lying flat on the freshly cut surface. The gouge is fed slowly forwards in a straight plane, and is held firmly down on the toolrest so it does not follow the work's uneven surface.

Hollowing the lid

To prevent the lid from splitting at some later date it must be made in the shape of a dome. This provides a

space into which the outer rim can shrink unobstructed.

You can use a large, round-nose scraper, fitted with an extra-long handle, to hollow the lid, but a ring tool will do the job more efficiently and give a cleaner finish. It allows you to cut in the direction of the grain, slicing through the fibres of the wood at their roots, leaving the surface fairly undisturbed, in contrast to the scraper which tends to break them off abruptly.

Start by positioning the tool horizontally, with the ring placed diagonally across the centre point of the workface. Angle the cutting edge of the ring into the work surface and slowly gyrate the tool to scoop out a small depression in the centre.

Repeat the cuts, using the toolrest as the point of axis, until you've formed a fair-sized hemisphere, at which stage you may turn the ring round so that it cuts with its reverse 45° edge. This alternative angle allows the tool to cut backwards up the sides of the hollow with the

bevel of the ring tool gliding over the freshly cut surface in the same way that a gouge is used. You may have to unclog the ring periodically to enable the tool to cut cleanly, but with practice you should soon be creating a continuous flow of shavings like fine spiral ribbons. To locate the lid onto the body of the chalice, cut a small, perfectly straight and parallel recess in the inside edge of the lid, using the corner of a square scraper.

To form the moulding around the edge of the lid, first part down with a parting tool about 20mm (¾in) from the end, so that you have a square section isolated from the rest of the workpiece. Then, with a 6mm (¼in) bowl gouge, cut two inverted quarter-round mouldings on each corner of the section.

I use a vertical toolpost made from a masonry nail fitted in a hole in the toolrest to support the back of the gouge for making its initial entry cuts into the side of the work. It's always at this point that the gouge is most likely to skid backwards and break up any crisp right-angle corner you are trying to produce. By pivoting the back of the gouge against this post, it can be held in place and then gyrated in an arc so that the concave shapes of the rim moulding are formed.

Lid cavity

Measure the depth of the lid cavity and mark this out on the outside of the cylinder. The area for the dome section of the lid is then isolated from the rest of the workpiece by making a parting cut about 10mm (⅜in) above the mark, to provide enough for the thickness of the lid.

After cutting a small step or fillet above the rim moulding, using the corner of the parting tool, the 6mm (⅜in) bowl gouge is then used to form the outside dome of the lid. Slowly feed the gouge around the curve of the dome, removing a small step of waste at each pass of the tool, and swing the handle in an arc so that the bevel follows the curved surface of the work.

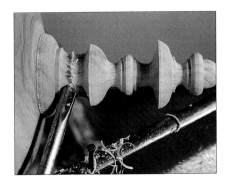

Photo 5 Cutting a hollow with a spindle gouge.

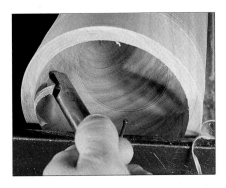

Photo 7 Slicing backwards up the wall of the chalice.

Cherry 'chalice' **95**

Test the lid thickness between your fingers after each pass of the gouge until it's even (6mm (¼in) at most), and reduce the area of cylinder nearest the chuck to expose a section of wood for the finial. The bulk of this waste can be removed with a roughing gouge before narrowing to a spout shape with the bowl gouge.

Remove the partially completed lid from the faceplate and complete work on the finial with the lid held in a jam chuck. This is made by carefully cutting a rebate on a scrapwood disc, so you produce a mandrel the precise size of the recess in the lid.

The sizing of the jam chuck is very important, because if you don't cut enough off you can split the lid trying to jam it on; cut too much off and lid will not be tight enough on the mandrel and can pop off during turning. Trim the section for the finial until it's the width of the widest moulding you intend to make, and then, from the top, round a section to form an acorn shape.

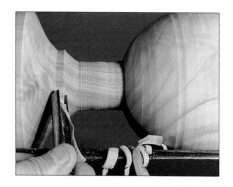

Photo 8 Forming a foot on the chalice with the bowl gouge.

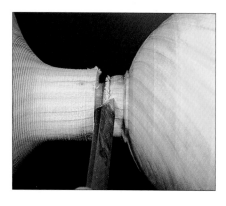

Photo 9 Cutting a bead with parting tool.

The convex curves and the steps and fillets forming the intersection points of the curved moulding are all cut with the standard 3mm (⅛in) parting tool. This is used by rolling it over on its side with the corner of the tool doing the work in true bead-making style, or by performing a simpler nibbling technique.

The small bead in the waist of the finial's stem is made in this way, by forming a square section first, which is then cut into an octagon section with the tool held at a wide angle. The final bead shape is achieved with the use of some coarse sandpaper. Cheating, you may say – but if it yields a good result...?

The concave hollows are formed with a miniature spindle gouge ground to a long, rounded point. To create the hollows, the tool is used on its side to start the cut and then, as the cut proceeds, twisted round so that it pans out at the bottom of the cove.

Sanding & polishing

Sand the lid smooth, starting with 150-grit abrasive for the wider areas, taking care not to rub away any of your crisp, carefully formed detail. Leave this for the finer 280 to 400-grit finishing grades. I use aluminium-oxide abrasive cloth, as it is especially flexible and can work in and out of the tightest hollows.

For a traditional finish which will improve with age, apply a coat or two of shellac French polish with a soft, clean, cotton cloth. Rub on a coat or two of soft fast-drying wax while the lathe is stationary, switch on and burnish with a soft cloth. For an even higher shine use carnauba wax, melting a layer on as the work rotates and burnishing with a soft cloth until you have a brilliant shine.

Chalice base

Process the log and attach one end in the chuck or screw it onto the faceplate. Slice the end clean, and carefully reduce the diameter so the lid fits snugly, but is not too tight. Hollowing is done in much the same

Photo 10 Applying carnauba wax and burnishing with a soft cloth.

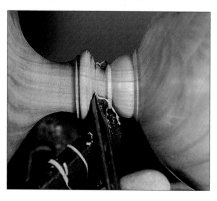

Photo 11 Decorating the stem with beads, ovolos, hollows and fillets.

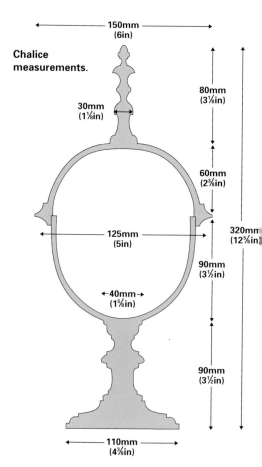

Chalice measurements.

150mm (6in)
30mm (1³⁄₁₆in)
80mm (3¹⁄₈in)
60mm (2³⁄₈in)
125mm (5in)
320mm (12⁵⁄₈in)
90mm (3½in)
40mm (1⁵⁄₈in)
90mm (3½in)
110mm (4³⁄₈in)

Photo 12 The end of the toolrest has been brought close for the delicate work of slicing down the stem's foot.

Photo 13 Hollowing the underside of the foot.

way as for the lid, but I used the Supertip hollowing tool (see panel) to form the cavity.

This tool, like the ring tool, has two cutting sides – one at an obtuse angle for cutting across the floor of the hollow, and another acute-angled edge for slicing backward up the chalice wall. The smaller radius of its edge, combined with the thicker, more rigid, shaft makes it more controllable than the ring tool when working deep at the bottom of the chalice hollow.

Mark the depth of the chalice on the outside, and part down with the parting tool to isolate the bowl of the chalice. Parting down on one side of a section in this way creates a corner which can be quickly sliced off and shaped with the gouge – and it also locates the intersection point between the base of the bowl and the stem of the chalice.

The bowl gouge is again used to form the narrow waist section of the

stem, slicing on its side so that the bevel works like the sole of a plane, regulating the depth of cut and preventing the tool edge from digging in.

I formed an ovolo moulding at the base of the bowl, using the parting tool. First I cut the square steps or fillets at each side of the quarter-round moulding, and then rounded off the middle square section and formed the convex quarter-round, using the rolling bead-cutting technique with the parting tool. Before proceeding all the way with the thin shape of the stem, which tends to weaken the support of the chalice's bowl, it's a good idea to finish sanding and polishing the bowl.

The end of the toolrest has been brought as close as possible to the work, to support the delicate procedure of slicing down the sweep of the stem's foot, which is then decorated with a series of small beads, ovolos, hollows and fillets.

If you have enough waste wood between the chuck jaws and the foot of the chalice, you can part the work off with a single continuous cut of the parting tool, or you may prefer to leave a section to hold the work and finish the parting off with a saw. This will leave a little hand work to the sole of the foot. I took my chalice out of the chuck and mounted it in a jam chuck, in a similar way to the lid, but brought up the tailstock to support the work, so the sole of the foot could be hollowed and trimmed safely. ■

Cup with lid removed.

The Supertip tool

The Supertip hollowing tool, designed by Roy Child and manufactured by Henry Taylor Tools Ltd, owes its origin to the hook tool, which has been used for centuries by hollow-vessel woodturners both in Britain and on the Continent. These were hand-forged (sometimes by the turner himself), the end of a shaft being first flattened and curved round to form a hook; then painstakingly sharpened by hand

with a slipstone, usually against the inside of the hook.
The Supertip has a replaceable tip made from high-speed steel, and keeps its edge far longer than the hand-forged hook tool. The tip screws into the end of a shaft of carbon steel and forms a flush fit, so there is nothing to catch on the toolrest or the walls of the workpiece. You get the same clean finish as with the ring tool, but the Supertip has the advantage that it can be worked right into the corner of a square-sided hollow. It can be sharpened on

Ring tool and Supertip hollowing tool.

conventional grinding equipment, although the acute cutting edge is better honed internally with a round diamond file.

Nest egg

An egg tree crafted from beautifully spalted, wet greengage

T his four-tier egg tree is designed to counter the tendency of wet wood to split when it dries out, which often happens when a shape contains a thick section of wood around the heart. It has three thin-walled shelves in the form of bowls, which can shrink in on themselves without splitting. A hole is drilled through the core of the tree, removing the pith and any small heart shakes, while also providing an additional shrinking space.

> ❝ **When** working with spalted timber it is even more important to wear a dust mask ❞

To make the rack, the centre of each end of the log is located and marked out with a pencil. This allows it to be accurately mounted between centres. Use a four-prong drive centre at the headstock end – driven securely home with a copper-headed hammer – and a revolving

centre in the tailstock. Set the lathe to its slowest speed of 500rpm (or less if you have the range), and turn the log down to a cylinder with the roughing-out gouge. When working with spalted timber it is more important than ever to wear an effective dust mask, because the fungal spores present in the wood are an additional health hazard to normal wood dust.

You will now need to prepare your work so that it can be held at one end. Use a 3mm (⅛in) parting tool, preferably fitted with an extra-long handle, to partially part through one end of the log, so that you form a flat surface on which to fix a faceplate. Rather than parting off completely, leave a short spigot the same diameter as the hole in the faceplate, so that it can be more easily centrally located.

Spalted wood is never as solid as sound, healthy timber, so you will need to use a lot more screws to hold the work securely. I use eight 38mm

(1½in) No.10 Spax screws to hold the work on the faceplate. These have machined, serrated threads which drive straight into the end of the log without the need for drilling pilot holes. You can of course use a compression chuck to hold the work on the lathe, which may be the only option if the wood is particularly soft. The advantage of a faceplate over a chuck is that it holds the work closer to the headstock, which reduces the risk of vibration occurring in the projecting workpiece.

Boring out the heartwood

To bore out the heartwood I use a 1¼in saw-toothed bit, fixed onto an extension bar, which is held in a drill chuck in the tailstock. I often find that when drilling into fibrous or very irregular-grained wood, the drill refuses to start cutting in the dead centre of the work. To get round this problem I start the hole, using a small square scraper, so that I have a shallow recess into which I can centrally locate the end of the drill. As you bore deeper into the body of the workpiece, remember to periodically withdraw the bit and clear the swarf from behind the cutting edge, as a heavy build-up can trap the drill in the work.

To hide the hole, you could turn a separate carrying handle or finial knob out of a piece of seasoned timber, but you must make the dowel of the finial slightly thinner than the

Photo 1 Roughing down the log.

Photo 2 Forming a flat end.

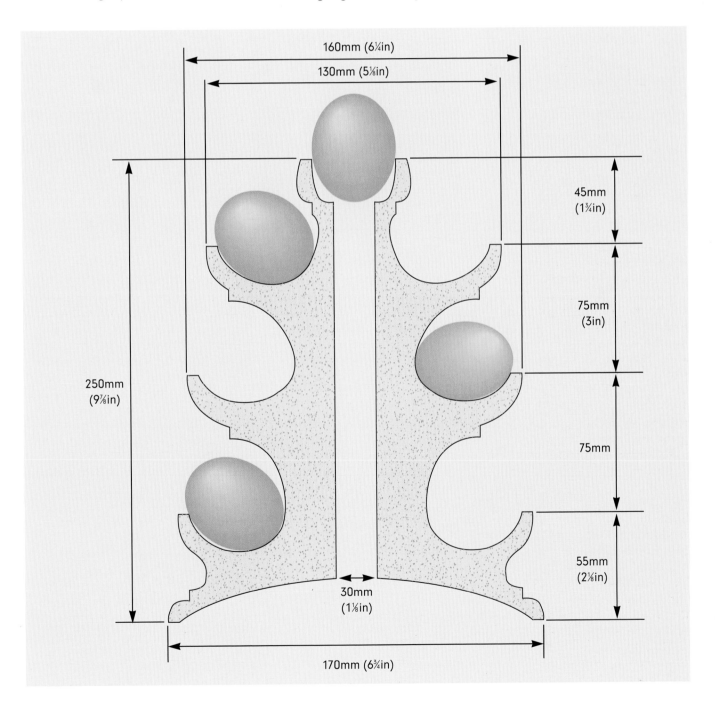

Photo 4 Withdrawing the saw-tooth bit to clear the swarf.

Photo 3 Boring out the centre.

Photo 5 Scraping out the top to form a cup.

Photo 6 Forming the spout shape, from which the top egg cup is turned.

hole to allow for shrinkage. A less problematic solution to hiding the hole is to widen it and form it into an egg cup. To form the cup, use a small round scraper, pointed slightly downwards from the horizontal, start cutting at the inside corner of the hole and work backwards towards the rim. With each cut, work the tool by slowly swinging the handle in an arc, stopping the lathe each time to try out the cup with an egg for size. I use a 13mm (½in) Superflute bowl gouge to reduce the diameter at the end of the workpiece and form a flat shoulder for hollowing out when forming the top shelf. The central spigot can then be shaped with a smaller gouge to form the outside of the egg cup.

It is when you come to hollowing out the bowl-like shelves of the egg tree that the real turning challenge of this project begins. With sound, un-

spalted timber it is possible to use a bowl gouge to hollow out the concave shelves, but this requires working directly into end grain, which tends to push the fibres of the wood back on themselves, producing a poor finish. The problem of broken end grain is magnified tenfold when the wood is as crumbly and loose-textured as this spalted fruitwood; and no amount of sanding will clean it up.

Loop hollowing tool

The solution is to use a tool which can reach into the back of the cavity and work backwards, cleanly slicing through the fibres at their root. My choice for this is the Supertip hollowing tool (as described on page 97). This tool has two cutting edges, one on each side, and two bevels: one which is almost at right angles

to the shaft, and the other at 45°. You should use the cutting edge with the right-angled bevel to cut at the bottom of the cavity and then change over to the 45° bevel when cutting backwards, up the inside wall of the hollow.

To hollow out the top bowl of the egg rack, start the cut at the centre point of the radius and work first in one direction and then the other, using the right-angled bevel edge of the loop tool. The tool is always used on its side so that the edge is presented at a near-vertical slicing angle and the bevel flush with the workface. To get the loop to cut, angle it so that the cutting edge dips into the surface of the workface, then slowly swing the handle in an arc around a point on the toolrest. You may have to un-clog the loop periodically to enable it to cut cleanly, but with practice you should soon be creating a continuous flow of shavings like fine spiral ribbons.

As you increase the depth of the semicircular cavity you will need to bring the 45° bevel edge into use. The 45° bevel is used when hollowing out deeper cavities. The angled cutting edge allows you to maintain a correct slicing action. Gently place the tool at the starting position of the previous cut and draw the tool through your fingers while making sure that the bevel glides over the freshly cut surface like the sole of a plane, preventing the tool's edge from digging in. Slowly swing the handle in a slow-motion arc, so that the bevel follows the curve of the hollow until the cutting edge of the tool emerges at the rim of the bowl. The tool is provided with a long handle for exerting the necessary leverage over the tool when

stretching beyond the direct support of the toolrest. The tool can equally be made to remove waste material quickly by taking heavy cuts, as it can perform the final finishing cuts required to create a smooth surface. On some fine-grained woods it is possible to obtain a finish straight from the tool so smooth that hardly any sanding is required.

I wanted the overall shape of my egg tree to taper inwards as it went up. To get this effect I started with the top shelf and made it as narrow as possible, so that it was just wide enough to hold a batch of eggs around the base of the centre egg cup. To size the cavity of the shelf, you will need to use a number of eggs to be sure that the hollow is big enough, but remember that eggs vary in diameter even after they have been classified as small, medium etc. You

need the walls about 3–4 mm (⅛–⁵⁄₃₂in) thick, so that they are strong enough to support the eggs, but not so thick that they cannot flex when they dry out and shrink.

Forming the shelves

The outside of the shelf can be created with a conventional bowl gouge, which can also be used to open up the tree for the next shelf down. The methods used for the top shelf can be employed when hollowing out the lower shelves of the egg tree. But the constricted working space between the shelves can cause a problem when it comes to forming a continuous curve of the central column where it intersects the base of the shelf and continues on inside the curve of the hollow. For this operation I have chosen an angled gouge, which has a bevel which is ground at an obtuse angle for working across the bottom of a cavity. It also has an inside flute which is especially angled to maintain a sharp cross section to the cutting edge. It is used in the same way as a conventional bowl gouge to slice round the outside curve of the shelves and to cut straight in to form a right-angled shoulder and to form the sides of the column.

Plinth decoration

The plinth of the egg tree has been decorated with a quarter-round moulding which is formed by cutting a square section at the edge of the base and then rounding it off in the same way as you would one side of a bead. I place the parting tool's edge so that it rests on the apex of the square section and then twist the handle so that the tool cuts with the corner and forms the round, as it is rolled over on its side. The same technique can be seen being used to form the bead around the top edge of the egg cup. A little clean-up operation may be required with a skew chisel at the intersection point where the round meets the small step or fillet.

Photo 7 A poor finish using a conventional bowl gouge

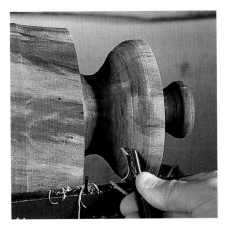

Photo 8 Slicing the outside shape with a bowl gouge

Photo 9 Back-slicing again in the lower shelf

Photo 10 The angled gouge, refining the shape of the middle tray

Photo 11 A deep cut with the angled gouge.

Photo 12 using a beading and parting tool to detail a round bead on the top egg cup.

Photo 13 Hollow the plinth and part nearly through.

Photo 14 Snap through the last remaining section with the lathe at rest and clean up the bottom.

Finishing

Spalted wood is often quite coarse in texture, but with care it is possible to preserve fairly crisp detail. When sanding, you will need to start off with some coarse abrasive to remove the last traces of tool marks. I use aluminium oxide abrasive that is resin-bonded onto a flexible cloth backing. I begin with 80 grit and follow through to 240 grit, which removes the scratches of the coarser abrasive. Finish off with 350 or 400 grit to be certain of obtaining a finish where the only marks visible on the work are the natural grain figuring of the timber.

Because of its probable contact with water, I have used a cellulose sealer to finish the egg tree. This is best brushed on all over quickly with a paintbrush, using a sheet of hardboard to protect the lathe bed from any splashes and

drops. Then before it dries, the whole surface of the work can be wiped with a clean cotton cloth. This will absorb any surplus polish and leave an even coat.

This method avoids the overlapping which can occur when the polish is applied with a cloth or rubber only (as used by French polishers), and can be repeated to create any thickness of finish required.

The egg tree is now ready to be parted off, and it is useful to have a parting tool fitted with a long handle. For this operation, make a series of angled cuts with the parting tool, in order to hollow out the base of the plinth, and also to get at a point beyond the end of the faceplate screws. Do not part all the way through to the core. Instead, stop just short and, with the lathe at rest, snap the egg stand off and clean up the base with a carving tool and abrasive. ■

Leaving dead trees like beech, hornbeam, birch and fruitwoods out in all weathers for a year or two produces a very colourful and striking effect in the timber. This is commonly known as spalting and is caused by the different kinds of fungal infections growing and spreading through the wet wood.

You do not want a wood blank to be soaking wet when you turn it or you will have problems sanding and polishing the finished work, so you really need to dry out the log to some extent by bringing it under cover for a week or so. This will also prevent further fungal growth.

If you are not going to make use of your stock of spalted wood straight away, you can preserve it by treating the ends of the logs with a paraffin-wax sealant to stop them splitting; and you can convert your wood into smaller blocks and discs at this stage.

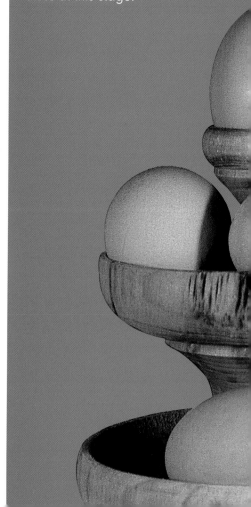

Spice whirl

This really, really useful revolving spice rack will keep all your spices in the same place, saving time and frustration

If you've ever lost a vital seasoning or spice when cooking for guests due to arrive in 10 minutes, this revolving spice rack may well be the answer. You can make a larger or smaller version by scaling up the size of the shelves, depending on the number of spice jars you want to store.

Spice jars at the back are brought to the front on rotating shelves by twisting the central column. This makes it just as effective inside the deep recess of a cupboard as when seated on an open shelf, and it can release precious space on a kitchen worktop.

The method I chose to hold the blank discs on the lathe requires you to drill each disc first with a central 22mm (⅞in) diameter hole. The best way to do this is on a drill press, which will ensure the hole runs at right angles through the axis of the disc. This is necessary if the disc is to run true on the wooden mandrel chuck, which is what you have to make next.

I make most of my wooden chucks from offcuts of beech, ash, or maple, but any regular-grained wood will do, provided it's fairly hard, dry and stable. These home-made chucking devices not only get round some ticklish turning problems, but are often the key to the work proceeding smoothly and trouble-free. Inventing and building one can be the most creative aspect of the job, especially with projects involving a lot of repetitive work.

This wedged-mandrel chuck makes it quick and easy to reverse and remount the workpiece on the lathe, so that work can be done each side in turn. To make it, fix a 100mm (4in) cube of hardwood onto a faceplate and turn it down to a 100mm (4in) cylinder, using a roughing-down gouge.

Make a large rebate in the cylinder by parting down with a parting tool about 25mm (1in) from the end of the block. Remove the waste with the gouge, leaving a 22mm (⅞in) diameter mandrel, slightly oversized so it can be trimmed more accurately with the beading and parting tool.

Wood list

I used sycamore – Europe's largest-growing maple, sometimes known as the great plane or great maple. It's a creamy-white, even-textured wood, delightful to turn. In for-mer days it was popular for making into household and dairy utensils, as it is nearly odourless, so it doesn't taint foodstuffs.

165mm x 25mm (6½ x 1in) discs for the base tray and top shelf (2 off)

305 x 38 x 38mm (12 x 1½ x 1½in) block for the column

A 75mm (3in) lazy-Susan mechanism is housed in a 125 x 25mm (5 x 1in) plinth.

Tools needed

19mm (¾in) roughing gouge
10mm (⅜in) bowl gouge
10mm (⅜in) spindle gouge
6mm (¼in) spindle gouge
3mm (⅛in) parting tool
10mm (⅜in) beading/parting tool
Round-nosed scraper
Depth gauge and vernier gauge
Faceplate
Wedged-mandrel chuck
22mm (⅞in) saw-toothed centre drill
Protective face shield.

1. Drilling the centre hole.

2. Mounting a blank disc on the wedged mandrel.

3. Driving home the wedge after fitting the disc onto the split mandrel.

A tip for getting the mandrel the right width is to reduce a short section about 1.5mm (¹⁄₁₆in) long at the end, which you can test out with one-off the discs before committing yourself to reducing the full length of the mandrel.

If the mandrel is made with an interference fit, the joint generated can be very strong on its own, without the wedge to enlarge it. This is OK for one-off jobs, but with repeated use the mandrel can become worn or compressed, and lose its effectiveness. To ensure a reliable grip is kept, saw a slot in the mandrel so that, after the disc has been fitted, a wooden wedge can be tapped in to expand the mandrel and hold the work secure.

Mechanism's house

Make the 125mm (5in) diameter plinth which houses the lazy-Susan mechanism first. Mount the disc onto the mandrel chuck and level off the face of the disc with a round-nosed scraper to form a flat base for the plinth. Test the face with a straightedge and then reverse the plinth and flatten off the other face.

To make the recess for the mechanism, part in at the middle of the disc to a depth of 6mm (¼in), using a beading and parting tool. Repeat this cut, gradually moving further away from the centre until you have a square-cornered cavity wide enough for the four corners of the lazy Susan to fit snugly against.

This will automatically locate the mechanism in the centre of the stand.

Use a 10mm (⅜in) bowl gouge to form the round sides of the plinth, placing it slightly on its side with the bevel in line with the direction of the cut, and then feeding it slowly across the corner of the disc. Two or three passes of the gouge will produce a chamfer, which, by gyrating the gouge handle in a slow arc as you cut, will transform into a quarter-round or ovolo moulding.

Bottom shelf

Mount the disc on the mandrel and flatten the face with the scraper, and then cut a shallow recess for

4. Cutting the recess in the plinth for the lazy-Susan mechanism.

5. Chamfering the side of the plinth.

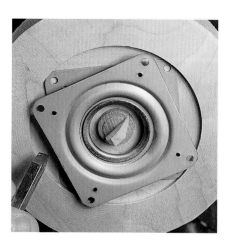

6. Testing that the mechanism fits snugly into the recess.

the lazy-Susan mechanism. Form a tight fit for the corners of the mechanism, as you did for the spice rack's stand. This will ensure that the spice rack's bottom shelf and plinth revolve on the same vertical axis when assembled.

Reverse the disc on the mandrel

7. Trimming the rim of the base shelf.

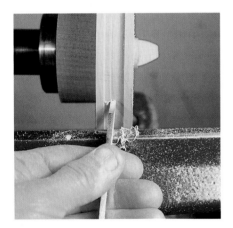

8. Forming the recessed frieze around the rim of the shelf.

and trim the outside edge with a 6mm (¼in) bowl gouge. To prevent the unsupported corner fibres being broken, work the gouge from both edges of the disc towards the middle of the rim.

The miniature bead and ovolo that form the decorative moulding on the sides of the shelf are formed in two stages, using a standard 3mm (⅛in) wide parting tool. First, make shallow parting cuts at right angles to the work, to block out the overall width and depth of the bead

and half-bead moulding. Then, with the same tool, chamfer and round off the square sections on the corners, using small angled parting cuts from side to side of the shape, to create the bead and ovolo mouldings.

To improve the finish and get a flat, even surface between the two beads, position the edge of the tool at a cutting angle, so that it only just lifts the fibres, and slowly slide it sideways, using just the corner of the blade to cut.

Fix the outer limits of the recess for the spice jars by first making two cuts with a narrow 3mm (⅛in) parting tool, and test them with a depth gauge to make sure they are equal in depth.

Then remove the bulk of the waste with a 10mm (⅜in) bowl gouge. Test the width with one of

9. Making the beads on the rim of the base shelf.

your spice jars and finish levelling the floor with a beading and parting tool. Use the lateral cutting technique with this tool to improve the finish.

Shape the central island of the tray by forming a quarter-round concave radius with a 10mm (⅜in) spindle gouge, ground with a long 'fingernail' edge.

Start by using the gouge on its side, and as you slice down, rotate it so that it pans out at the base of the curve.

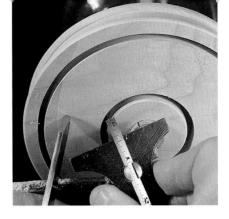

10. Using a gauge to check the depth and level of the floor.

11. Cutting away the waste.

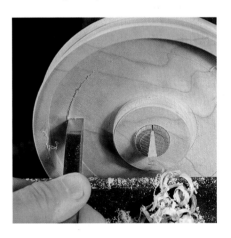

12. Levelling off the floor using a lateral cut with a beading and parting tool.

13. Forming a radius on central island.

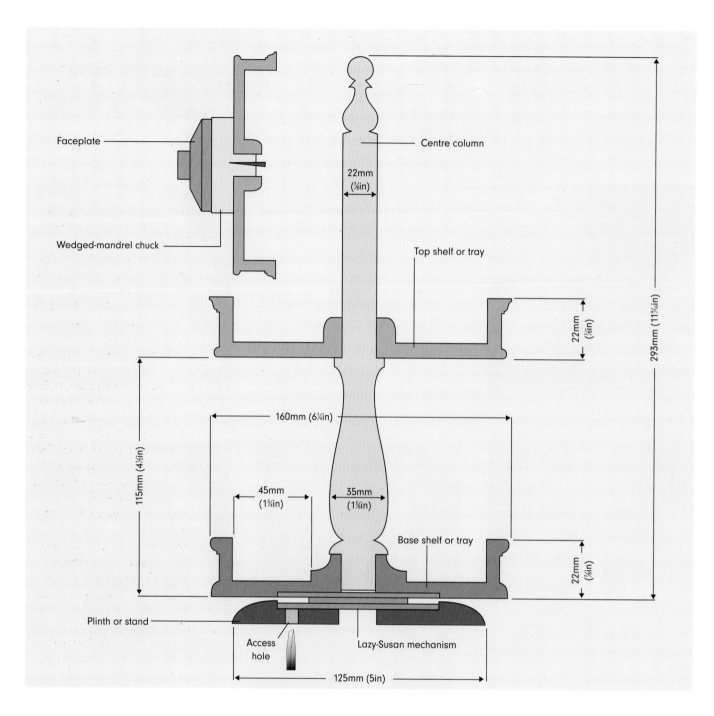

Faceplate

Wedged-mandrel chuck

Centre column

22mm
(⅞in)

Top shelf or tray

293mm (11⅝in)

22mm
(⅞in)

160mm (6¼in)

115mm (4½in)

45mm
(1¾in)

35mm
(1⅜in)

Base shelf or tray

22mm
(⅞in)

Plinth or stand

Access
hole

Lazy-Susan mechanism

125mm (5in)

Top shelf

The top shelf is made in the same way as the bottom one, except that it does not need a recess for the lazy-Susan mechanism. I have rounded the central island to form a convex moulding and used a classical cornice design around the edge of the shelf. This is first blocked out in a series of steps with the parting tool as before, and then a small spindle gouge is used to form the tiny convex and concave curves of the cornice moulding.

14. Forming an ogee moulding around the edge of the top shelf.

Central column

Fit the square section for the column between centres and rough it down to a cylinder. Cut a dowel 25mm long by 22mm diameter (25 x ⅞in) at one end, to form the joint at the bottom of the column and connect it to the base of the spice rack. Allow enough height beneath the top shelf for the loading and unloading of the spice jars, and cut into the column with the parting tool to form the rebate which supports the top shelf.

15. Using the roughing gouge to shape the neck of the central column.

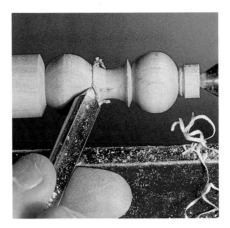

17. Shaping the neck of the top of the column.

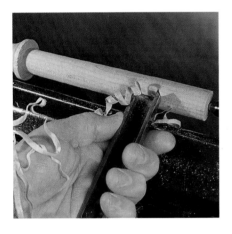

16. Forming the cylindrical spindle of the top half of the column.

18. Parting off the work.

Sanding & polishing

To sand, I use aluminium-oxide abrasive cloth, which is especially flexible and works in and out of the tightest hollows. When sanding each part of the spice rack, start with 150-grit abrasive for the wider areas. Avoid rubbing away crisp detail by leaving these sections for the finer 280 to 400-grit finishing grades. Lightly rub with 350 or 400 grit to erase the scratches of the coarser grades. You should now have a surface where the only marks visible on the work are in the natural grain figuring of the timber.

I used a cellulose sealer to finish the spice rack, because of its possible contact with water. For an even coat, apply this quickly with a brush (using a sheet of hardboard to protect the lathe bed from splashes), then, before the sealer dries, wipe off the surplus with a clean cotton cloth. This method avoids the overlapping which can occur when the polish is applied with just a cloth or rubber. Repeat after the first coat has dried to create a thicker finish if required.

To assemble the spice rack, fix the lazy Susan into the recess in the plinth with four short screws, and drill a hole through the plinth to allow a screwdriver to pass through, then screw in the screws for the base shelf. The other parts are glued together with a strong epoxy.

And there you have it! You will now have all the spices you need for cooking at your fingertips. ■

To make the traditional vase shape on the lower half of the column, start by slicing a V-cut about 6mm (¼in) from the base with the corner of the beading and parting tool, and round the shoulders to form the ovolo and convex base of the vase. The hollow waist of the vase is then shaped with the roughing gouge. Reduce the diameter above to a 22mm (⅞in) parallel spindle which will pass through the hole in the top shelf.

To form the decorative top of the column and provide the revolving spice rack with a knob to carry and rotate the shelves, bring the toolrest up as close as you can and make three V-cuts 13mm, 32mm and 63mm (½, 1¼, and 2½in) from the top of the spindle.

Remove the waste above the end-most V-cut with a 3mm (⅛in) parting tool and form the ball shape between the two top Vs by repeatedly rolling the parting tool over on its side and cutting with the corner of the blade.

Use a spindle gouge to hollow out the neck of the finial. As you shape the curve of the hollow, you will need to restrict the cutting area of the tool to just its tip, because any more contact with the cutting edge can cause the tool to dig in. After sanding and polishing, part the column by slicing through above the ball with the beading tool.

Ready for assembly.

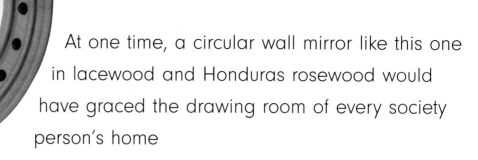

At one time, a circular wall mirror like this one in lacewood and Honduras rosewood would have graced the drawing room of every society person's home

Mirror of society

Circular wall mirrors date back to the early half of the 19th century. As a guest at a posh dinner party, you might have seen a fine, gilded example, complete with a pair of carved candle sconces, hanging above the head of the table, reflecting in its convexity the whole room. The butler would stand to one side, to see at a glance if a plate needed to be removed or a wine glass filled.

Work out the design on paper before you start, as the front and back sectional details must meet precisely to provide adequate room for the mirror plate and backing board. I drew a full-scale drawing of the frame section on a piece of card and carefully calculated the proportions of the decorative mouldings and rebates so that they all went together. This produced the maximum amount of curvature, and ensured there was enough strength in the frame as well.

Producing such a design on paper or card before you start can also help overcome any unforeseen hitches, and provide a useful tool on which to work out an alternative scheme.

As my design card shows, the original mirror frame was to have small

First design, with whole spheres.

Collet chuck.

Modified design, with buttons.

Mirror plate

Back board

12mm (½in)

15mm (⅝in)

60mm (2⅜in)

20mm (¾in)

25mm (1in)

1 The design stage.

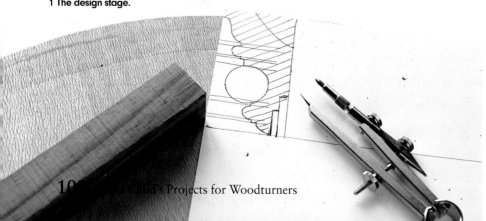

wooden spheres set into a deep concave recess. I drew this design before I had fully taken into account the pronounced warp in the disc, which when flattened out would seriously reduce its thickness. But the card helped me to quickly convert the design to one with semicircular buttons applied to a bevelled part of the frame instead of the complete spheres.

Big jam chuck

The large chucking device shown below provides a really effective method of holding this wide frame around its outer rim without marking. For this 350mm (13¾in) frame you need to cut out a 420mm (16½in) circle of 16mm (⅝in) thick MDF on the bandsaw and glue a 30mm (1⅛in) wide border of 20mm (¾in) thick pine blocks around the disc's perimeter.

When the glue has dried, find the centre and fix the chuck onto a face flat, so it can be mounted on the lathe.

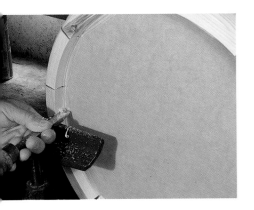

2 Trimming the jam chuck.

Set the lathe speed to 500 rpm or less, and gently trim the inside surface of the blocks to produce a deep, parallel-sided rebate into which the mirror frame can be firmly pressed. Don't worry if you make the chuck opening too wide to obtain a really tight interference fit – you can always put some cardboard packing in the gap and fit some retaining blocks to keep the frame secure.

When using the jam chuck you must ensure the workpiece is pressed firmly against the concentric back surface of the chuck, and that the retaining blocks make contact with the surface of the frame when they are screwed up tight. An over-tight fitted frame can be extracted from the chuck by means of a softwood wedge driven into the gaps between the side blocks.

Mounting the disc

To make a large frame which will not twist or shrink into an oval shape after completion, you will need a large disc of well-seasoned, quarter-sawn timber. This straight-grained piece of London plane or lacewood (the name given when it has its characteristic flecked figuring) is ideal.

After planing one side flat on the workbench, the simplest way to hold the workpiece on the lathe is to screw the blank to an intermediate disc of 13mm (½in) plywood or chipboard. The screws must be positioned carefully, so that they screw into the thickest section of the mirror frame, or they may appear through the front of the frame when the mouldings are cut.

3 Screwing the disc to a faceplate, enlarged with a disc of chipboard.

An alternative method of holding the work onto the disc is to use double-sided adhesive tape. Apply the tape to both surfaces, and burnish it down with the back of a screwdriver handle. When the two sticky surfaces come together, a strong grip is produced. You can make it even stronger by crimping in the bench vice or going round the edge with a G-cramp squeezing the two discs together.

Find the centre of the intermediate disc and screw the metal faceplate in position. Now select a suitable lathe speed. If you are unfamiliar with turning large diameters on your lathe, work at the slowest speed to start with and then, if this seems too slow, move it up a notch. I found 500rpm worked well for this size of disc.

When turning a wide-diameter project, it helps to have a lathe with a swivelling headstock, so that the work can be rotated in line with the lathe bed. This enables you to stand in a safe, comfortable, well-balanced position relative to the workpiece, without having to stretch awkwardly across the lathe bed or compromise with the cutting angle of the tools. It also rotates the disc in line with the length of the lathe bench, which provides more rigidity for the work.

It is especially important when turning wide-diameter work to wear a face shield, as the speed generated at the rim of the disc is much faster than with thin spindle work.

Frame section

Form the flat face and square sides of the overall cross section of the frame first, which can then be marked out with the beads and intersections of the moulding positions. The simplest way to face off the disc is to use a series of light cuts with a round scraper, sliding

4 Flattening off the front of the disc with a round scraper.

the knuckle of your forefinger against the back of the toolrest to help guide the cut in a flat plane. Test the surface with a straightedge and use a flat sanding block at the back of the abrasive when you sand the face smooth.

It is not safe to use a wide-bladed tool on the rim of a disc, so put your scraper away and square off the outer edge of the disc using a 6mm (¼in) or 10mm (⅜in) bowl gouge. Hold the gouge handle down, close to your hip bone, so you get a good cutting angle.

Line up the tool bevel with the square side of the rim and feed it across, so it slices through the surface, removing a thin section of wood in one steady, controlled, movement. Work from the front edge to the middle of the rim, and then from the back edge to the middle, so the disc corners are not broken away.

Rather than turning away the central section of the disc with a bowl gouge, thereby wasting a perfectly good 230mm (9in) diameter disc which could be used for another project, I parted through the face of the disc with a standard 3mm (⅛in) parting tool.

Mark out the full extent of the frame section and feed the parting tool slowly into the face at a 45° cutting angle, taking two parallel cuts so the blade doesn't bind in the groove. Make your cut about 3mm (⅛in) in from the line, so the little bit of waste can be cleaned up with the corner of a square scraper.

I usually part all the way through, holding the tool in one hand and switching off the lathe with the other, at the point where the waste disc comes away. One of the advantages of using the double-sided tape to hold the work is that the centre is safely fixed against the back of the faceplate and can be prised away after parting through, when the lathe is stationary.

Forming the moulding

To form hollows, beads and other intricate shapes on the edge of a wide disc, you need a different set of techniques from those used to create the moulded decoration for a chair or leg spindle. For on a disc which has been cut out of a plank you will get two distinct grain directions. Slice-cutting with the skew chisel to make V-cuts is unsuitable and unsafe here.

the wood, must be slowed to a snail's pace to allow for the full rotation of the workpiece to elapse before the edge of the tool can be moved on.

This lateral cutting movement of the tool is used whenever possible, as it helps to obtain good finishes on the mouldings. To work out the direction of the cut, think 'woodcarving' and cut with the grain as much as possible, so that the grain fibres are not broken back on themselves.

Use your template card to mark up the frame into the various intersection points of the mouldings. I use my handy pair of odd-leg callipers, which is a very accurate method of transferring dimensions from the template to the workpiece.

Reduce the frame section into a series of steps and smaller square sections which sets out the overall perimeters of the beads and

5 Squaring off the rim of the disc with the gouge.

7 Using the 1/1 scale drawing to set out the dimensions on the workpiece.

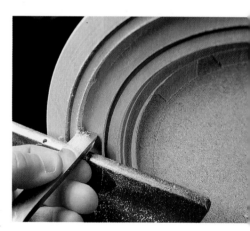

8 Cutting the square core dimensions of the mouldings.

6 Parting through the face of the disc to remove the waste in one piece.

I use the beading and parting tool, standard parting tool and spindle gouge like scrapers, but instead of holding them horizontally, tilt them slightly upright at a cutting angle. Using tiny cuts, I rely on the tool's keen edge to obtain clean finishes. This calls for even more tool honing on the oilstone than usual.

If I *do* use a rolling technique with the parting tool to produce a bead, I keep in mind the large diameter of the disc and the increased amount of cutting that this involves. The lateral movement of the tool, to get the corner to slice through the fibres of

9 Rounding off the convex section of the ogee moulding with the parting tool.

10 Forming a bead using the corner of the parting tool again.

12 Drilling the fixing holes for the buttons using the drill jig.

mouldings. Use the lateral cutting technique when you form the rounds of the beads, and also when hollowing the concave area of the ogee moulding, which is cut with the point of the spindle gouge.

You are now free to sand the work smooth and polish the front of the frame by brushing cellulose sanding sealer into the grooves and crevices of the mouldings. Quickly, before the sealer has time to dry, wipe away the surplus with a clean cloth. Then, with the lathe running, rub some carnauba wax onto the high points of the mouldings and burnish them up with a soft flannelette cloth.

Button decoration

The twenty-four 13mm (½in) Honduras rosewood buttons which form part of the decoration of the frame are made by first reducing the square block of rosewood to a cylinder. These cylinders are held in a collet chuck. To make this chuck, select a seasoned block of hardwood and screw it to a faceplate. If you want the chuck to be re-usable at a later date, recess the faceplate into the back of the block before securing it with the screws.

Turn the block to a cylinder and flatten the face by slicing across with a gouge. Taper the outside, leaving the thickness of the sides 4mm ($\frac{5}{32}$in) at the end, and saw the chuck along its length to form eight equal jaws.

Cut the collar out of a scrap of 15mm ($\frac{5}{8}$in) plywood so that it slides over the tapered body of the chuck

and compresses the jaws together. The head of each button is domed over with the parting tool and the dowel cut at rear. After sanding and polishing it is parted off, ready for the next section of the cylinder to be moved along and turned.

Indexing ring

To space the buttons equally around the frame, I have rigged up my own indexing device using a Masterchuck indexing ring. This ring is jam-fitted onto a wooden sleeve which is then hot-glued to the back of the faceplate. A twist drill acts as the arm of the indexing jig, which is held down with my thumb to a block of wood which projects from the side of a small table cramped to the lathe bed.

11 The indexing ring is hot-glued to the back of the faceplate.

Button dowel holes

The indexing jig works in collaboration with the drilling jig, which ensures the holes are at the same angle. To make the drill jig, drill a hole, the same size as the dowels, squarely through a block of hardwood using the drill press.

Hold the block between centres and turn a spigot which fits firmly in the toolrest banjo. To set the jig, feed the drill through the hole in the block and position it so that its point is at the same height as the lathe centre, then set it at right angles to the bevel on the mirror frame. After the first hole has been drilled, turn the frame to the new position and drill each hole in turn.

To make the recesses for the mirror plate and back board, remove the

frame from the backing plate by undoing the screws or by slowly forcing the double-sided tape apart, and cut the rebate for the mirror plate and back board. This is done with the parting tool, with the frame held securely in the large jam chuck.

After gluing the buttons, fit the mirror plate in position, and glue the backing board in place with a little piece of soft tissue or foam in between to support the back of the plate. A brass ring or plate fixed in the back to suspend the mirror from is all that's needed to complete the assembly. ∎

13 Cutting the recess for the mirror plate in the back of the frame.

14 Forming the domed head of the rosewood button

Rest easy

An Elizabethan joint stool is a useful exercise in many of the basic woodturning shapes

Oak stools similar to the one featured were originally made about 400 years ago. The simple design of the leg incorporates many of the basic woodturning shapes. There is a round bead, small step or fillet, tapered pillar, and an ogee or vase shape. Square sections feature at the top and bottom to house the mortice and tenon joints for the frame rails.

Choosing the design

When it comes to design, I am happy to modify existing styles and decoration to suit my needs. Traditional forms are not just pleasing to the eye, they are usually easier to copy.

1 Hold the work on the lathe between the end shoes

2 Make a parting cut through the corners of the workpiece

3 Twist the tool on its side to avoid catching the corners with the gouge

Preparing the legs

To prepare the legs, plane and thickness the square sections, cut them to length and line them up together side by side. Mark out the central section, which will be turned, and the areas at the top and bottom, which will remain square. Score round the lines with a knife so that later on, when the corners are parted through, any splintering with the tool will occur only on the waste side of the cut.

Mounting legs

The usual way to mount a spindle on the lathe is first to draw lines across the ends from corner to corner to find the centre point, then to punch with the drive centre on that mark. The problem with this method is that the point of the drive centre nearly always wanders off centre slightly when it is punched. This is not important if the work is then completely reduced to a cylinder, but an off-centre spindle will show up if the workpiece includes square sections.

A more accurate method of holding the work on the lathe is to make a pair of end shoes. These simple chucking devices are turned out of bits of waste wood to form circular cups or shoes that squeeze accurately over each square end of the leg. One cup is made on a faceplate to go on the drive end of

the lathe and the other is made with a central hole, which sits on the revolving tailstock.

Part through corners

As with all turning operations you should wear eye protection, and this is especially important with this kind of between-centres turning, because you will be looking directly into the line of fire of the shavings and splinters.

> 66 When it comes to design, I am happy to modify existing styles and decoration to suit my needs. Traditional designs are usually easier to copy 99

With the lathe set to about 2000rpm, use a standard 3mm (⅛in) parting tool to part through the square corners of the leg. Hold the tool at right angles to the axis of the work and slowly feed it forwards, withdrawing after each cut. Be careful not to catch the corners to each side. I always draw it towards the waste wood side so that if it does do any damage, it will be to the corner that is going to be removed.

The blur caused by the revolving corners makes it difficult to see clearly when the cut is complete. Stop the lathe from time to time to check your progress – go too deep

with the parting tool and you will end up with an ugly score mark in the work. I like to leave the sides of the square section slightly uncut so that I can be sure that I am using the full width of the leg.

Removing waste

Use a roughing gouge to remove the corners of the middle area of the leg and form it into a cylinder. With the toolrest set parallel to the work, slide your knuckles against it, using it like a fence so that the spindle thickness is kept to the same width all the way along. When cutting away the waste next to the square end sections, turn the gouge over onto its side so that it does not catch in the square corners. Any damage at this stage is irreparable.

Marking out the work

To mark out the intersection points of the various beads and hollows that make up the design, I have made a full-scale drawing of the leg on the edge of a piece of card so that the proportions of the design can be worked out before turning starts. This template is held against the side of the cylinder, and the four lines which mark out the pattern on this joint-stool leg – two for the bead, one for the bottom of the tapered pillar and one for the base of the ogee vase shape – are copied across.

4 Using a template is an easy way to transfer the shape when making copies

5 Slice the pommel with a round-edged skew chisel

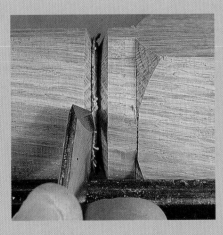

6 Slice the V-cut, working from both sides until the required depth is achieved

Pommel-making

Before making the decorative mouldings at each end of the leg, use a 12mm (½in) skew chisel to slice the square corners at an angle to make pommels. To perform this cut in a wood as hard as oak, you will need to grind a very acute angle on the edge of the tool, which should then be honed until it is razor-sharp.

With the longest point of the blade resting on the toolrest, feed the point into the ends of the revolving corners at a slight angle – the action is a bit like taking a slow-motion snooker shot into the corner hole. It is vital that only the point makes contact with the work because if any of the blade catches then the tool will be dragged sideways and slide out of control.

Chip off the extreme corners first and then repeat the cut as many times as it takes by slicing a little bit further back each time until you have completed the pommel. The point of the tool should intersect at the bottom of the square section where it meets the cylinder. Tidy up the area at the base of the pommel with a few light passes with the parting tool.

V-cuts

Turning furniture details requires a methodical, step-by-step approach. After forming the cylinder, the first stage for the leg mouldings is to slice V-cuts, one at the top side of the bead and another directly below the ogee shape. Use the skew chisel again; feed the point into the work on one side of the line and then repeat the same cut – in mirror image – on the other side of the line.

> Turning furniture details requires a methodical, step-by-step approach

Enlarge the V by taking further slice cuts, making sure that the point of the tool meets at the bottom of the previous cut each time and you remove the waste section. I always try to simplify my design as much as possible by making all the V-cuts at the same angle and depth. The cuts do not need to be particularly deep for quite full shapes to be formed around them.

Forming the bead

Use a standard parting tool to part down and isolate the section of cylinder which is to be made into the bead at the top of the leg. The bead can then be formed in the salient point between the V and the parting cut.

First place the parting tool so that the corner rests on the apex of the cylinder bead section. Then slowly twist the handle using a wrist action so that the corner of the tool's edge engages with the surface of the work and then cuts away the shoulder as the tool rotates. With subsequent cuts of the same kind, more of the shoulder is removed so that the semi-circular shape of the bead is formed. This is then repeated in the opposite direction to form the other side of the bead.

Forming vase hollow

A vase or peardrop-shape moulding forms the decoration at the base of the leg. The neck or hollow of the vase moulding is created using a 9mm (⅜in) spindle gouge. By slicing down from each side of the slope with this tool on its side, and twisting it so that it pans out at the bottom, a smooth curving radius is formed. The bulb of the vase can then be rounded using the parting tool to complete the shape.

Vertical toolpost

The spindle gouge is also employed to form the small radius at the top of the leg, below the bead. There is a small square section or fillet directly below the bead, which needs to be preserved, and I use a small vertical toolpost made out of a masonry nail. This is placed in a hole drilled in the top of the toolrest and acts as a fulcrum on which to rest the back of the gouge as it makes its entry cut.

To form the tapered middle area of leg, take the spindle roughing gouge and sharpen it to give it a fresh edge.

7 Forming the bead with a standard parting tool

8 Hollowing the neck of the ogee vase shape with a spindle gouge

9 Rounding off the base of the ogee profile with a parting tool

Before finishing the taper, examine the surface of the work for signs of roughness and broken grain, then, if necessary, improve the finish by honing a sharper edge on your gouge and making a series of very fine, delicate finishing cuts.

Sanding

When sanding, start with coarse abrasive to remove the last traces of tool marks. Gouge ripples on the long taper and the apex of the vase shape can be removed by rubbing with a piece of fresh abrasive. The areas in the deep hollows and on the steep sides of shapes, consisting of end grain, are quite a different story.

The finish that you achieve with these surfaces depends entirely on whether they have been sliced cleanly with the tools in the first place. Attempting to sand away such faults as side gashes, torn grain or uneven radiuses is likely to cause added faults, such as rounded detail and friction splits.

The abrasive I use is aluminium oxide, resin-bonded onto a flexible cloth. I start off with 80-grit and follow up with 240, which removes the scratches of the former abrasive. With oak you can usually polish after the 240-grit, but I normally give the work a light rub with 350 or 400-grit to be certain of obtaining a clean finish.

The legs are now ready to be morticed for the top and bottom rails.

Finishing

Leave the finishing of the legs until after the stool has been joined together. This is because some final hand-sanding is nearly always required to remove excess adhesive, and also because any polished surface would be vulnerable to being bruised by the sash cramps used to hold the assembly together while the glue sets.

When it comes to choosing a finish for oak furniture, I am a bit of a traditionalist and prefer French polish, beeswax and oil finishes to the newer plastic-based ones. Even if they do not stand up to hot coffee or water staining, they allow the wood to mellow and develop a patina, which deepens and becomes richer with age.

> " I am a bit of a traditionalist and prefer French polish, beeswax and oil finishes "

To apply shellac polish, make up a small rubber out of a piece of old woollen sock, rolled into a ball and wrapped round with some pure cotton cloth. The best cloth for French polishing is flannelette, as this has a thick, soft pile and spreads the polish evenly. You will need a number of prepared pieces of this as it wears out quite quickly. You should also put on a pair of thin

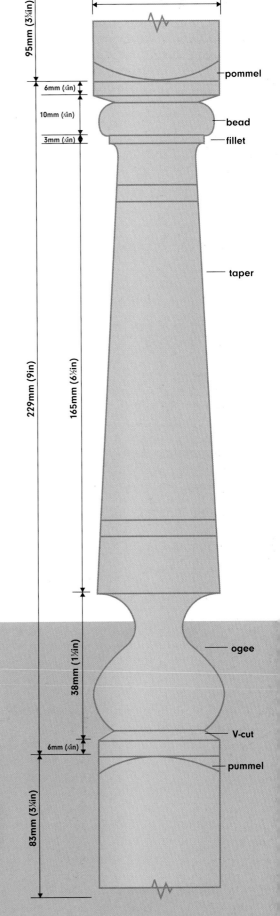

- 95mm (3¾in)
- 47mm (1⅞in)
- pommel
- 6mm (¼in)
- bead
- 10mm (⅜in)
- fillet
- 3mm (⅛in)
- taper
- 229mm (9in)
- 165mm (6½in)
- ogee
- 38mm (1½in)
- V-cut
- 6mm (¼in)
- pummel
- 83mm (3¼in)

drawing not to scale

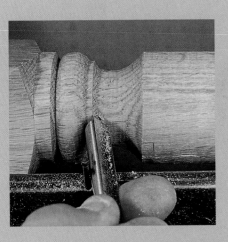

10 Forming the small radius using the vertical toolrest

11 Forming the taper on the leg

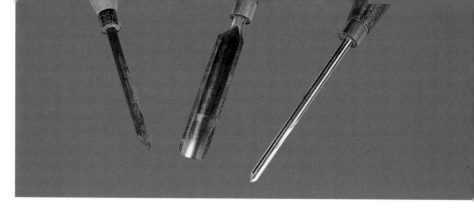

From the left, a standard 3mm (⅛in) parting tool, 19mm (¾in) roughing-down gouge and 9mm (⅜in) spindle gouge

rubber gloves if you don't want to end up with French-polished hands.

Polished performance

Dip the rubber in a saucer of polish, squeeze out the surplus polish and rub a layer all over the stool, working it into the mouldings and inside corners. Don't be too worried if the finish is a bit uneven at this stage, but avoid drips or heavy build-ups of wet polish.

As soon as an area becomes sticky, leave it alone and move over to a fresh part of the frame. You may need to leave the work for a few minutes for the polish to go off a bit, before wiping on a second coat in the same way.

Keep adding layers of shellac in this way until the wood is completely sealed and a thin layer of polish covers the stool. Before rubbing down or applying wax, leave the polish to harden. This can take anything up to a week, depending on the temperature in the workshop. To tell when the polish is properly dry, rub it with some 600-grit abrasive. If the finishing cloth clogs, the stool will have to wait a day or two longer.

On the other hand, if a fine white dust comes off, the polish is ready for further treatment.

Rub all over the surface lightly with the abrasive and then add another coat of shellac using a freshly made rubber, or simply go straight over to the final waxing. ∎

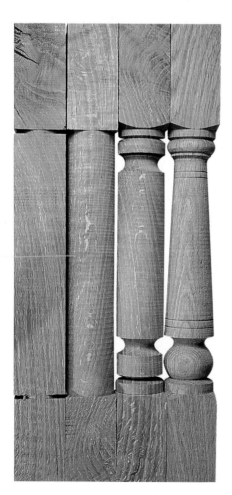

Four stages for four legs

The finished oak stool

About the author

Woodturning has been part of Chris Child's life since the age of 10, and at a 17th-century farmhouse in north Essex he continues the teaching and writing tradition which was started nearly half a century ago by his father, Peter Child.

Chris left school in the early 1970s and, like so many young people with an affinity for the arts and crafts, wanted an occupation which would enable him to make full use of his natural hand skills. During his early years as an antique furniture restorer he learnt to recognise and appreciate the traditional furniture styles of the past, and these have been an important influence on his work ever since. One of his first commissions was to turn an exact copy of a pair of figured walnut candlesticks that were part of the collection in the Victoria and Albert Museum. With only a photograph for reference, he worked painstakingly, taking the best part of a day to make the first candlestick, but it was while struggling with the twin that he finally began to develop a more methodical approach and to adopt many of the techniques that he still finds effective today.

The kind of first-hand experience gained from undertaking projects like this, as well as a wide variety of others, has given him the confidence to teach and demonstrate this fascinating craft to students of all ages, abilities and walks of life. The two-day course which he has run at his studio-workshop since 1984 has started hundreds of people off on a new hobby, and produced some well-recognised figures in the woodturning world as well. He has been a regular contributor to many woodwork magazines in the UK and USA.

When it comes to woodturning, although a traditionalist at heart, Chris is always looking for the best and the easiest way to achieve a satisfactory result, which means having an open mind to new developments in tool technology. In this field he is not alone in benefiting from the innovative work that has been achieved by his brother Roy, having on more than one occasion tested out one of the latest gouge designs or advanced tool systems.

The Old Hyde
Little Yeldham
Halstead
Essex
CO9 4QT
Tel: 01787 237291
Fax: 01787 238522

TITLES AVAILABLE FROM
GMC Publications
BOOKS

WOODTURNING

Adventures in Woodturning	David Springett
Bowl Turning Techniques Masterclass	Tony Boase
Chris Child's Projects for Woodturners	Chris Child
Colouring Techniques for Woodturners	Jan Sanders
Contemporary Turned Wood: New Perspectives in a Rich Tradition	
	Ray Leier, Jan Peters & Kevin Wallace
The Craftsman Woodturner	Peter Child
Decorating Turned Wood: The Maker's Eye	Liz & Michael O'Donnell
Decorative Techniques for Woodturners	Hilary Bowen
Illustrated Woodturning Techniques	John Hunnex
Intermediate Woodturning Projects	GMC Publications
Keith Rowley's Woodturning Projects	Keith Rowley
Making Screw Threads in Wood	Fred Holder
Turned Boxes: 50 Designs	Chris Stott
Turning Green Wood	Michael O'Donnell
Turning Pens and Pencils	Kip Christensen & Rex Burningham
Useful Woodturning Projects	GMC Publications
Woodturning: Bowls, Platters, Hollow Forms, Vases,	
Vessels, Bottles, Flasks, Tankards, Plates	GMC Publications
Woodturning: A Foundation Course (New Edition)	Keith Rowley
Woodturning: A Fresh Approach	Robert Chapman
Woodturning: An Individual Approach	Dave Regester
Woodturning: A Source Book of Shapes	John Hunnex
Woodturning Jewellery	Hilary Bowen
Woodturning Masterclass	Tony Boase
Woodturning Techniques	GMC Publications

WOODCARVING

Beginning Woodcarving	GMC Publications
Carving Architectural Detail in Wood: The Classical Tradition	
	Frederick Wilbur
Carving Birds & Beasts	GMC Publications
Carving the Human Figure: Studies in Wood and Stone	Dick Onians
Carving Nature: Wildlife Studies in Wood	Frank Fox-Wilson
Carving on Turning	Chris Pye
Decorative Woodcarving	Jeremy Williams
Elements of Woodcarving	Chris Pye
Essential Woodcarving Techniques	Dick Onians
Lettercarving in Wood: A Practical Course	Chris Pye
Making & Using Working Drawings for Realistic Model Animals	
	Basil F. Fordham
Power Tools for Woodcarving	David Tippey
Relief Carving in Wood: A Practical Introduction	Chris Pye
Understanding Woodcarving in the Round	GMC Publications
Useful Techniques for Woodcarvers	GMC Publications
Woodcarving: A Foundation Course	Zoë Gertner
Woodcarving for Beginners	GMC Publications
Woodcarving Tools, Materials & Equipment (New Edition in 2 vols.)	
	Chris Pye

WOODWORKING

Advanced Scrollsaw Projects	GMC Publications
Beginning Picture Marquetry	Lawrence Threadgold
Bird Boxes and Feeders for the Garden	Dave Mackenzie
Celtic Carved Lovespoons: 30 Patterns	Sharon Littley & Clive Griffin
Celtic Woodcraft	Glenda Bennett
Complete Woodfinishing	Ian Hosker
David Charlesworth's Furniture-Making Techniques	David Charlesworth
David Charlesworth's Furniture-Making Techniques – Volume 2	
	David Charlesworth
The Encyclopedia of Joint Making	Terrie Noll
Furniture-Making Projects for the Wood Craftsman	GMC Publications
Furniture-Making Techniques for the Wood Craftsman	GMC Publications
Furniture Restoration (Practical Crafts)	Kevin Jan Bonner
Furniture Restoration: A Professional at Work	John Lloyd
Furniture Restoration and Repair for Beginners	Kevin Jan Bonner
Furniture Restoration Workshop	Kevin Jan Bonner
Green Woodwork	Mike Abbott
Intarsia: 30 Patterns for the Scrollsaw	John Everett
Kevin Ley's Furniture Projects	Kevin Ley
Making Chairs and Tables	GMC Publications
Making Chairs and Tables – Volume 2	GMC Publications
Making Classic English Furniture	Paul Richardson
Making Heirloom Boxes	Peter Lloyd
Making Little Boxes from Wood	John Bennett
Making Screw Threads in Wood	Fred Holder
Making Shaker Furniture	Barry Jackson
Making Woodwork Aids and Devices	Robert Wearing
Mastering the Router	Ron Fox
Pine Furniture Projects for the Home	Dave Mackenzie
Practical Scrollsaw Patterns	John Everett
Router Magic: Jigs, Fixtures and Tricks to	
Unleash your Router's Full Potential	Bill Hylton
Router Tips & Techniques	Robert Wearing
Routing: A Workshop Handbook	Anthony Bailey
Routing for Beginners	Anthony Bailey
Sharpening: The Complete Guide	Jim Kingshott
Sharpening Pocket Reference Book	Jim Kingshott
Simple Scrollsaw Projects	GMC Publications
Space-Saving Furniture Projects	Dave Mackenzie
Stickmaking: A Complete Course	Andrew Jones & Clive George
Stickmaking Handbook	Andrew Jones & Clive George
Storage Projects for the Router	GMC Publications
Test Reports: The Router and Furniture & Cabinetmaking	
	GMC Publications
Veneering: A Complete Course	Ian Hosker
Veneering Handbook	Ian Hosker
Woodfinishing Handbook (Practical Crafts)	Ian Hosker
Woodworking with the Router: Professional	
Router Techniques any Woodworker can Use	
	Bill Hylton & Fred Matlack

UPHOLSTERY

The Upholsterer's Pocket Reference Book — David James
Upholstery: A Complete Course (Revised Edition) — David James
Upholstery Restoration — David James
Upholstery Techniques & Projects — David James
Upholstery Tips and Hints — David James

TOYMAKING

Scrollsaw Toy Projects — Ivor Carlyle
Scrollsaw Toys for All Ages — Ivor Carlyle

DOLLS' HOUSES AND MINIATURES

1/12 Scale Character Figures for the Dolls' House — James Carrington
Americana in 1/12 Scale: 50 Authentic Projects — Joanne Ogreenc & Mary Lou Santovec
Architecture for Dolls' Houses — Joyce Percival
The Authentic Georgian Dolls' House — Brian Long
A Beginners' Guide to the Dolls' House Hobby — Jean Nisbett
Celtic, Medieval and Tudor Wall Hangings in 1/12 Scale Needlepoint — Sandra Whitehead
Creating Decorative Fabrics: Projects in 1/12 Scale — Janet Storey
The Dolls' House 1/24 Scale: A Complete Introduction — Jean Nisbett
Dolls' House Accessories, Fixtures and Fittings — Andrea Barham
Dolls' House Furniture: Easy-to-Make Projects in 1/12 Scale — Freida Gray
Dolls' House Makeovers — Jean Nisbett
Dolls' House Window Treatments — Eve Harwood
Easy to Make Dolls' House Accessories — Andrea Barham
Edwardian-Style Hand-Knitted Fashion for 1/12 Scale Dolls — Yvonne Wakefield
How to Make Your Dolls' House Special: Fresh Ideas for Decorating — Beryl Armstrong
Make Your Own Dolls' House Furniture — Maurice Harper
Making Dolls' House Furniture — Patricia King
Making Georgian Dolls' Houses — Derek Rowbottom
Making Miniature Chinese Rugs and Carpets — Carol Phillipson
Making Miniature Food and Market Stalls — Angie Scarr
Making Miniature Gardens — Freida Gray
Making Miniature Oriental Rugs & Carpets — Meik & Ian McNaughton
Making Period Dolls' House Accessories — Andrea Barham
Making Tudor Dolls' Houses — Derek Rowbottom
Making Victorian Dolls' House Furniture — Patricia King
Miniature Bobbin Lace — Roz Snowden
Miniature Embroidery for the Georgian Dolls' House — Pamela Warner
Miniature Embroidery for the Tudor and Stuart Dolls' House — Pamela Warner
Miniature Embroidery for the Victorian Dolls' House — Pamela Warner
Miniature Needlepoint Carpets — Janet Granger
More Miniature Oriental Rugs & Carpets — Meik & Ian McNaughton
Needlepoint 1/12 Scale: Design Collections for the Dolls' House — Felicity Price
New Ideas for Miniature Bobbin Lace — Roz Snowden
The Secrets of the Dolls' House Makers — Jean Nisbett

CRAFTS

American Patchwork Designs in Needlepoint — Melanie Tacon
Beginning Picture Marquetry — Lawrence Threadgold
Blackwork: A New Approach — Brenda Day
Celtic Cross Stitch Designs — Carol Phillipson
Celtic Knotwork Designs — Sheila Sturrock
Celtic Knotwork Handbook — Sheila Sturrock
Celtic Spirals and Other Designs — Sheila Sturrock

Complete Pyrography — Stephen Poole
Creative Backstitch — Helen Hall
Creative Embroidery Techniques Using Colour Through Gold — Daphne J. Ashby & Jackie Woolsey
The Creative Quilter: Techniques and Projects — Pauline Brown
Cross-Stitch Designs from China — Carol Phillipson
Decoration on Fabric: A Sourcebook of Ideas — Pauline Brown
Decorative Beaded Purses — Enid Taylor
Designing and Making Cards — Glennis Gilruth
Glass Engraving Pattern Book — John Everett
Glass Painting — Emma Sedman
Handcrafted Rugs — Sandra Hardy
How to Arrange Flowers: A Japanese Approach to English Design — Taeko Marvelly
How to Make First-Class Cards — Debbie Brown
An Introduction to Crewel Embroidery — Mave Glenny
Making and Using Working Drawings for Realistic Model Animals — Basil F. Fordham
Making Character Bears — Valerie Tyler
Making Decorative Screens — Amanda Howes
Making Fabergé-Style Eggs — Denise Hopper
Making Fairies and Fantastical Creatures — Julie Sharp
Making Greetings Cards for Beginners — Pat Sutherland
Making Hand-Sewn Boxes: Techniques and Projects — Jackie Woolsey
Making Knitwear Fit — Pat Ashforth & Steve Plummer
Making Mini Cards, Gift Tags & Invitations — Glennis Gilruth
Making Soft-Bodied Dough Characters — Patricia Hughes
Natural Ideas for Christmas: Fantastic Decorations to Make — Josie Cameron-Ashcroft & Carol Cox
New Ideas for Crochet: Stylish Projects for the Home — Darsha Capaldi
Papercraft Projects for Special Occasions — Sine Chesterman
Patchwork for Beginners — Pauline Brown
Pyrography Designs — Norma Gregory
Pyrography Handbook (Practical Crafts) — Stephen Poole
Rose Windows for Quilters — Angela Besley
Rubber Stamping with Other Crafts — Lynne Garner
Sponge Painting — Ann Rooney
Stained Glass: Techniques and Projects — Mary Shanahan
Step-by-Step Pyrography Projects for the Solid Point Machine — Norma Gregory
Tassel Making for Beginners — Enid Taylor
Tatting Collage — Lindsay Rogers
Tatting Patterns — Lyn Morton
Temari: A Traditional Japanese Embroidery Technique — Margaret Ludlow
Trip Around the World: 25 Patchwork, Quilting and Appliqué Projects — Gail Lawther
Trompe l'Oeil: Techniques and Projects — Jan Lee Johnson
Tudor Treasures to Embroider — Pamela Warner
Wax Art — Hazel Marsh

GARDENING

Alpine Gardening — Chris & Valerie Wheeler
Auriculas for Everyone: How to Grow and Show Perfect Plants — Mary Robinson
Beginners' Guide to Herb Gardening — Yvonne Cuthbertson
Beginners' Guide to Water Gardening — Graham Clarke
Big Leaves for Exotic Effect — Stephen Griffith
The Birdwatcher's Garden — Hazel & Pamela Johnson
Companions to Clematis: Growing Clematis with Other Plants — Marigold Badcock
Creating Contrast with Dark Plants — Freya Martin
Creating Small Habitats for Wildlife in your Garden — Josie Briggs
Exotics are Easy — GMC Publications
Gardening with Hebes — Chris & Valerie Wheeler
Gardening with Shrubs — Eric Sawford

MAGAZINES

WOODTURNING ◆ WOODCARVING ◆ FURNITURE & CABINETMAKING
THE ROUTER ◆ NEW WOODWORKING ◆ THE DOLLS' HOUSE MAGAZINE
OUTDOOR PHOTOGRAPHY ◆ BLACK & WHITE PHOTOGRAPHY
TRAVEL PHOTOGRAPHY ◆ MACHINE KNITTING NEWS
KNITTING ◆ GUILD OF MASTER CRAFTSMEN NEWS

The above represents a full list of all titles currently published or scheduled to be published.
All are available direct from the Publishers or through bookshops, newsagents and specialist retailers.
To place an order, or to obtain a complete catalogue, contact:

GMC Publications,
166 High Street Lewes East Sussex BN7 1XU United Kingdom
Tel: 01273 488005 Fax: 01273 478606
E-mail: pubs@thegmcgroup.com

Orders by credit card are accepted